应用型本科院校"十二五"规划教材/经济管理类

Business English

商贸英语

主　编	刘忠梅	程　芳
副主编	朱玉琴	李明明
	姚　娜	姜　颖
	耿莉莉	韩　梅
	刘莹莹	

哈尔滨工业大学出版社
HARBIN INSTITUTE OF TECHNOLOGY PRESS

内容简介

全书共13章,主要分为外贸理论和外贸口语两大部分。外贸理论部分内容包括国际贸易政策、国际贸易方式、服务贸易、国际贸易壁垒、支付和进出口货物物流活动等;外贸口语部分主要介绍了商务会晤、产品推介、商务会餐以及商务旅行四个方面内容。本教材具有实用性、知识性和时效性的特点,编写体例简洁明了、深入浅出。

本书可供应用型本科院校经济贸易专业的本科高年级学生使用,也可供对外贸易业务人员和各类涉外企业相关人员自学使用。

图书在版编目(CIP)数据

商贸英语/刘忠梅,程芳主编. —哈尔滨:哈尔滨工业大学出版社,2012.8

应用型本科院校"十二五"规划教材

ISBN 978－7－5603－3694－7

Ⅰ.①商… Ⅱ.①刘…②程… Ⅲ.①商务-英语-高等学校-教材 Ⅳ.①H31

中国版本图书馆 CIP 数据核字(2012)第 167425 号

策划编辑	赵文斌 杜 燕
责任编辑	常 雨
出版发行	哈尔滨工业大学出版社
社　　址	哈尔滨市南岗区复华四道街10号 邮编150006
传　　真	0451－86414749
网　　址	http://hitpress.hit.edu.cn
印　　刷	黑龙江省委党校印刷厂
开　　本	787mm×960mm 1/16 印张 12 字数 258 千字
版　　次	2012年8月第1版 2012年8月第1次印刷
书　　号	ISBN 978－7－5603－3694－7
定　　价	21.80 元

(如因印装质量问题影响阅读,我社负责调换)

《应用型本科院校"十二五"规划教材》编委会

主　任	修朋月　竺培国
副主任	王玉文　吕其诚　线恒录　李敬来
委　员	（按姓氏笔画排序）

丁福庆　于长福　马志民　王庄严　王建华
王德章　刘金祺　刘宝华　刘通学　刘福荣
关晓冬　李云波　杨玉顺　吴知丰　张幸刚
陈江波　林　艳　林文华　周方圆　姜思政
庹　莉　韩毓洁　臧玉英

序

哈尔滨工业大学出版社策划的《应用型本科院校"十二五"规划教材》即将付梓,诚可贺也。

该系列教材卷帙浩繁,凡百余种,涉及众多学科门类,定位准确,内容新颖,体系完整,实用性强,突出实践能力培养。不仅便于教师教学和学生学习,而且满足就业市场对应用型人才的迫切需求。

应用型本科院校的人才培养目标是面对现代社会生产、建设、管理、服务等一线岗位,培养能直接从事实际工作、解决具体问题、维持工作有效运行的高等应用型人才。应用型本科与研究型本科和高职高专院校在人才培养上有着明显的区别,其培养的人才特征是:①就业导向与社会需求高度吻合;②扎实的理论基础和过硬的实践能力紧密结合;③具备良好的人文素质和科学技术素质;④富于面对职业应用的创新精神。因此,应用型本科院校只有着力培养"进入角色快、业务水平高、动手能力强、综合素质好"的人才,才能在激烈的就业市场竞争中站稳脚跟。

目前国内应用型本科院校所采用的教材往往只是对理论性较强的本科院校教材的简单删减,针对性、应用性不够突出,因材施教的目的难以达到。因此亟须既有一定的理论深度又注重实践能力培养的系列教材,以满足应用型本科院校教学目标、培养方向和办学特色的需要。

哈尔滨工业大学出版社出版的《应用型本科院校"十二五"规划教材》,在选题设计思路上认真贯彻教育部关于培养适应地方、区域经济和社会发展需要的"本科应用型高级专门人才"精神,根据黑龙江省委书记吉炳轩同志提出的关于加强应用型本科院校建设的意见,在应用型本科试点院校成功经验总结的基础上,特邀请黑龙江省9所知名的应用型本科院校的专家、学者联合编写。

本系列教材突出与办学定位、教学目标的一致性和适应性,既严格遵照学科体系的知识构成和教材编写的一般规律，又针对应用型本科人才培养目标及与之相适应的教学特点，精心设计写作体例，科学安排知识内容，围绕应用讲授理论，做到"基础知识够用、实践技能实用、专业理论管用"。同时注意适当融入新理论、新技术、新工艺、新成果，并且制作了与本书配套的PPT多媒体教学课件，形成立体化教材，供教师参考使用。

《应用型本科院校"十二五"规划教材》的编辑出版，是适应"科教兴国"战略对复合型、应用型人才的需求，是推动相对滞后的应用型本科院校教材建设的一种有益尝试，在应用型创新人才培养方面是一件具有开创意义的工作，为应用型人才的培养提供了及时、可靠、坚实的保证。

希望本系列教材在使用过程中，通过编者、作者和读者的共同努力，厚积薄发、推陈出新、细上加细、精益求精，不断丰富、不断完善、不断创新，力争成为同类教材中的精品。

黑龙江省教育厅厅长

前　言

随着对外经济贸易往来和交流活动的日益增多,对复合型商务人才的需求也越来越大,同时也对从事或即将从事国际商务活动人员的专业知识和外语素质提出越来越高的要求。近年来,商贸英语的应用已经在经济、生活和工作中日益扩大,并已经成为各经贸高等学院教学的一门重要专业课程。

作者经过认真筛选,提供了原汁原味的经贸英语文章,题材兼顾中外经济,涵盖诸多行业领域。《商贸英语》主要分为外贸理论和外贸口语两大部分。外贸理论部分内容包括国际贸易政策、国际贸易方式、服务贸易、国际贸易壁垒、支付和进出口货物物流活动等;外贸口语部分主要介绍了商务会晤、产品推介、商务会餐以及商务旅行四个方面内容。

本教材具有实用性、知识性和时效性的特点,尤为重要的是对课文中出现的各种专业组织和专业词汇进行了更加深入广泛的补充性解释。本书不仅能提高学生的英语运用能力,还能提高学生阅读理解商贸英语文章的水平,为其日后工作打下必要的语言基础。同时,本书也可作为涉外活动人士用于提高商务英语水平的阅读材料。

本书由刘忠梅、程芳主编,全书共13章,具体分工如下:第1章由姜颖编写;第2章由姚娜编写;第3、8章由朱玉琴编写;第4、5章由李明明编写;第6、9章由刘忠梅编写;第7章由耿莉莉编写;第10章由韩梅编写;第11章由刘莹莹编写;第12、13章由程芳编写。

由于作者水平有限,编写中难免存在疏漏和不足,欢迎读者结合实际学习和应用情况提出宝贵意见并加以指正,以便进一步补充修订。

编　者
2012年6月

Contents

Chapter 1	Current International Trade	1
Chapter 2	The Goals and Instruments of International Trade Policy	14
Chapter 3	Modes of International Trade	29
Chapter 4	International Trade in Services	42
Chapter 5	Free Ports and Foreign-Trade Zones	54
Chapter 6	International Trade Barrier	73
Chapter 7	The Sino-U. S. Trade Relation	85
Chapter 8	Terms of Payment	99
Chapter 9	Transport and Logistics	112
Chapter 10	Meeting People	127
Chapter 11	Product Presentation	139
Chapter 12	Business Dinner	152
Chapter 13	Business Travel	167

Chapter 1

Current International Trade

> **Pre-reading questions:**
> 1. Do you have an idea about international trade?
> 2. What are the important reasons for international trade?
> 3. Could you briefly explain the theory of absolute advantage and the theory of comparative advantage?
> 4. What problems does international trade bring about?
> 5. What's the developing trend of international trade?

Text

Introduction

International trade, also known as world trade, foreign trade or overseas trade, is the fair and deliberate exchange of goods (trade in goods) and exchange of services (trade in services) across national boundaries. It concerns trade operations of both import and export and includes the purchase and sale of both visible and invisible goods, the former of which is called trade in goods while the latter of which is called trade in services.

A country's development level of foreign trade reflects a nation's opening degree and degree of dependence to the world economy. A country's foreign trade turnover as compared with its Gross Domestic Product (GDP) calls the degree of dependence of economy to foreign trade. So, it is our most important and basic work in our opening-up to the outside world to participate in international trade actively. We should pay much attention to the study and research of international trade, and grasp its characteristic and developing trend.

Reasons for International Trade

1. Resource reasons

The uneven distribution of resources around the world is one of the basic reasons why nations began and continue to trade with each other.

(1) Favorable climatic conditions and terrain

Climatic conditions and terrain are very important for agricultural produces. The difference in these factors enables some countries to grow certain plants and leaves other countries with the only choice to import the products they consume. For example, Colombia and Brazil have the ideal climate for growing coffee beans but other countries don't. Then Colombia and Brazil have the opportunity to export coffee beans and coffee to countries worldwide. Another example is that the U.S. Great Plains states have the ideal climate and terrain for raising wheat. This has made the U.S. a big wheat exporter.

(2) Natural resources

Some countries are the major suppliers of certain natural resources because the distribution of natural resources around the world is somewhat haphazard. The Middle East, for instance, has rich oil reserves and is the main source of oil supply to the world. It has over 50% of the world total reserves and produces about 40% of the world total output. Over 2/3 of the oil that West Europe and Japan need is imported from the Middle East and the U.S. oil military consumption in Europe and Asia is largely purchased from that area.

(3) Skilled workers

U.S., Japan, and western European countries have skilled workers who are able to manufacture sophisticated equipment and machinery such as jet aircrafts and computers, etc. Other countries, since they don't have well-trained engineers and workers, must import the equipment from these countries.

(4) Capital resources

Developing countries need to modernize their industries and economies with advanced machinery, equipment and plant that they are not yet able to manufacture because of the lack of capital. This has given rise to the need for developing international trade.

(5) Favorable geographic location and transport costs

There are many examples that countries have developed close economic relationships chiefly because they are geographically close to each other. Sino-Japanese trade relationship is to some degree determined by geographic proximity and low transport cost. U. S. and Canada have a very close trade relationship for similar reasons. E. U. can be another example.

(6) Insufficient production

Some countries cannot produce enough items they need. U. K., for instance, does not have a large enough agricultural population. In fact, only 5% of its population is engaged in agriculture and they mainly grow fruits and flowers. U. K. then has to import 60% of its total agricultural consumption.

Developing countries normally do not have enough manufactured goods as they need and therefore have to import them.

2. Economic reasons

In addition to getting the products they need, countries also want to gain economically by trading with each other. It is made possible by varied prices for the same commodity around the world, reflecting the differences in the cost of production.

(1) Absolute advantage — by Adam Smiths in *The Wealth of Nations* (1776)

Smith assumed that each country could produce one or more commodities at a lower real cost than its trading partners. It then follows that each country will benefit from specialization in those commodities in which it has an "absolute advantage," (i. e. being able to produce at a lower real cost than another country), exporting them and importing other commodities which it produces at a higher real cost than does another country.

(2) Comparative advantage — by David Ricardo in *Principles of Political Economy* (1871)

Ricardo showed that absolute cost advantages are not a necessary condition for two nations to gain from trade with each other. Instead, trade will benefit both nations provided only that their relative costs, that is, the ratios of their real costs, are different for two or more commodities. In short, trade depends on differences in comparative cost, and one nation can profitably trade with another even though its real costs are higher (or lower) in every commodity.

A country has a comparative advantage if it can make a product relatively more cheaply than other countries. A country should make the product that yields it the greatest advantage or the least comparative disadvantage.

This theory is the basis of specialization and trade.

3. Political reasons

Political objectives can sometimes outweigh economic considerations between countries. One country might trade with another country in order to support the latter's government which upholds the same political doctrine. Or trade with some countries is banned or restricted just not to benefit a government with political disagreements.

Benefits of Interactional Trade

1. Cheaper goods

For one thing, countries trade because there is a cost advantage. This has been explained in the section of "economic reason" for international trade. Further, competition in the world market remains constant. This has made prices even lower. Last, if the quality of the imported goods is better but the price is not higher compared with the domestic cost, there is still a cost advantage.

2. Greater variety when goods come from more countries

Anyone who has experienced China's economic development in the past decades can tell the changes in the variety of both capital goods and consumer goods. These changes have not only improved the quality of our life but also increased the productivity of our industries.

3. Wider market with increasing number of trading partners

International trade can greatly expand the market. The expansion enables manufacturers to take advantage of economies of scale in both research and production. Besides, since markets around the world are often in different development stages, newly expanded markets can help extend the life of products.

4. Growth of economy

Foreign trade has become more and more important for many countries as it creates jobs that have both economic and political significance. Thus, countries have attached increasing importance to foreign trade. For economies that are highly dependent on foreign trade, it is crucial for them to keep foreign trade growing to ensure the development of the economies.

Problems in International Trade

1. Trade restrictions

Despite the benefits that all countries can receive from international trade, various kinds of restrictions on trade among countries are very common today.

(1) Reasons for trade restrictions

First, many countries want a diversified economy to be less dependent on foreign countries both economically and politically.

Then, it is crucial for countries to protect their vital industries, which are closely related to stability and economic development. For instance, during 18th—19th centuries, Britain's production cost of cotton products was greater than China's and India's, but Britain protected and continued its textile industry. Right after the Second World War, Japan's cost of steel industry was greater than that of the U.S.. Now the American's cost of steel production is bigger than Japan's. Yet neither of them has allowed free competition in this crucial industry.

Thirdly, there is an infant industry argument which maintains that a new industry needs to be protected until the labor force is trained, the production techniques are mastered and the operation becomes large enough to enjoy the economies of scale and to be able to compete in the market. It is not fair to let an industry in its infant stage to compete with a mature industry.

Furthermore, domestic jobs need to be protected from cheap foreign labor, especially for labor-intensive industries such as textile industry, since employment is crucial to a country's stability.

Last, there are pure political reasons. There have been always examples that some countries refuse to do business with other countries because of political reasons.

(2) Kinds of restrictions

According to the time of collection, duties can be divided into import duty and export duty. Besides regular import duty, importers might have to pay import surtax, too. In addition to tariffs, countries also use other methods to make import more difficult. Quota is a quantitative restriction or upper limit in terms of physical quantity or value. An import license is a permit for import, which can be independent or combined with quotas. Foreign exchange control intends to control import by limiting the access to foreign money that is needed for imports. State monopoly of import and export, import and export are restricted by giving exclusive authorities of import and export to only a limited number of (state) companies. There are other forms of non-tariff barriers and countries are continuing to create more.

2. Cultural problems

There are two major cultural issues that contribute to the success of international trade, the first aspect is language, including terms of transaction, and the other aspect is customs and manners.

3. Monetary conversion

Since different currencies are involved in international trade, conversion between currencies is inevitable. Yet it is no simple job to convert one currency into another without a loss while almost all currencies float every minute. Similar to cultural problems, this issue needs to be addressed by other books due to its complication.

Current International Trade Situation and Developing Trend

1. worldwide

The knowledge economy is penetrating constantly every area in the whole world, and the process of the globalization of world economy is accelerating the further development of international economy and trade. So, there are some new characteristics in the development of international trade, for example, the new changes and characteristics in the developing speed of international trade, the changes of structure in the international trade, the equilibria of development in international trade, the integrity of regional economy, and so on. International trade also demonstrate some new trend at the same time. The trade of high technology-intensive products will increase sharply, E-commerce and network trade will become the mainstream of trade way, management trade is growing fast, the technological barrier will become the main means of trade protection, the dispute of the intellectual property right will become the main dispute in international trade, ect. Facing the opportunity and challenge in international trade. Our country should take relevant countermeasures actively; fully utilize the favorable factors in international environment to promote economy development of our country.

2. China's overseas trade situation

The State Council Information Office has arranged a news conference about China's overseas trade. Vice Minister of Commerce, Fu Ziying introduced China's efforts to stabilize its imports and exports amid an unfavorable external economic environment.

Fu Ziying said despite a slump in exports, the market share for Chinese products has increased in international markets. He pointed out that more signs indicate a recovery for the Chinese economy, but as the global economic situation remains uncertain, China's exports still face downward pressure.

He said China will continue its policy to stabilize external demand and optimize export structures. He added that China would also encourage domestic companies to go abroad and cooperate with international partners. Facing the opportunity and challenge in international trade, our country should take relevant countermeasures actively; fully utilize the favorable factors in international environment to promote economy development of our country.

Vocabulary

deliberate *adj.* 故意的
intentional or planned

exchange *n.* 交换
when you give something to someone and they give you something else

dependence *n.* 依赖，依靠
rely on, depend on
when you need something or someone all the time, especially in order to continue existing or operating

uneven *adj.* 不平均的
not level, equal, flat or continuous

distribution *n.* 分布
the way in which people or things are spread out in a place

terrain *n.* 地形
an area of land, when considering its natural features

produce *n.* 生产
to make something or bring something into existence

somewhat *adv.* 稍微，有点
slightly

haphazard *adj.* 偶然的，随意的
not having an obvious order or plan

reserve *n.* 储备
a reserve is a supply of something that is available for use when it is needed

sophisticated *adj.* 复杂的
a sophisticated machine, device, or method is more advanced or complex than others

modernize *v.* 使现代化
to make something more modern

Sino-Japanese *adj.* 中国及日本的，中日的

insufficient *adj.* 不足的，不够的
not enough
proximity *n.* 接近，亲近
the state of being near in space or time
economically *adv.* 节约地；节省地
using little money, time, etc
assume *v.* 假定
to accept without verification or proof
specialization *n.* 专业化
a particular area of knowledge or the process of becoming an expert in a particular area
yields *v.* 生产
to supply or produce something positive such as a profit, an amount of food or information
outweigh *v.* 在重量上超过；比……重要
to be greater or more important than something else
uphold *v.* 维持；赞成；支撑
to defend or keep a principle or law, or to state that a decision which has already been made, especially a legal one, is correct
doctrine *n.* 教条，学说
ban *v.* 禁止
to forbid (= refuse to allow), especially officially
competition *n.* 竞争
when someone is trying to win something or be more successful than someone else
expansion *n.* 扩大
when something increases in size, number or importance
significance *n.* 重要性
importance
attach *v.* 认为……具有
to fasten, join or connect; to place or fix in position
crucial *adj.* 关键的，极其重要的
extremely important or necessary

diversified *adj.* 多样化的，多元化的
to become more varied or different

levy *v.* 征税，收税
an amount of money, such as a tax, that you have to pay to a government or organization

quantitative *adj.* 数量(上)的
relating to numbers or amounts

stipulate *v.* 规定
to state exactly how something must be or must be done

complication *n.* 复杂，错杂
something which makes a situation more difficult, or when it does this

penetrate *v.* 渗入
to move into or through something

equilibrium (复数 equilibria) *n.* 均衡，均势

mainstream *n.* (思想或行为的)主流
considered normal, and having or using ideas, beliefs, etc which are accepted by most people

Phrases

compare with	(把……)与……相比；比得上
pay ... attention to	注意
enables ... to ...	使能够，使可能
give rise to	引起，导致
to some degree	在某种程度上
in addition to	除……之外
take advantage of	利用
be related to	和……有联系
be dependent on	依靠，依赖
be engaged in	从事于

Key terms

visible goods	有形商品
invisible goods	无形商品
trade turnover	贸易成交额
Gross Domestic Product (GDP)	国内生产总值
commodity	商品
productivity	生产率
an infant industry	新生工业,幼稚工业,新兴产业
labor force	劳动力
labor-intensive	劳动力密集
technology-intensive	技术密集
technological barrier	技术壁垒
intellectual property right	知识产权
capital goods	资本货物
consumer goods	消费品
tariff	关税
levy	征收
import/export duty	进/出口关税
import surtax	进口附加税
dumping	倾销
anti-dumping duty	反倾销税
variable levy	差价关税
non-tariff barriers	非关税壁垒
quota	配额
import license	进口许可证
monopoly	垄断
government procurement	政府采购

Post-Reading Activities

I. Answer the following questions based on what you have read in the text.

1. What are the important reasons for international trade?
2. Why do many countries impose restrictions on trade?
3. What is tariff? How can tariff be classified? Please name at least 4 types of tariff.
4. What are non-tariff barriers? Please name at least 8 types of non-tariff barriers.
5. Could you briefly explain the theory of absolute advantage and the theory of comparative advantage?
6. What benefits does international trade bring about?

II. Look at the terms in the left-hand column and find the correct definitions in the right-hand column. Copy the corresponding letters in the blanks.

1. _____ levy		A.	when you give something to someone and they give you something else
2. _____ exchange		B.	an amount of money, such as a tax, that you have to pay to a government or organization
3. _____ quota		C.	a permit for import, which can be independent or combined with quotas
4. _____ import license		D.	a quantitative restriction or upper limit in terms of physical quantity or value
5. _____ diversified		E.	intends to control import by limiting the access to foreign money that is needed for imports
6. _____ foreign exchange control		F.	to become more varied or different

III. Translate the following sentences into Chinese.

1. Instead, trade will benefit both nations provided only that their relative costs, that is, the ratios of their real costs, are different for two or more commodities.

2. These changes have not only improved the quality of our life but also increased the productivity of our industries.

3. Thirdly, there is an infant industry argument which maintain that a new industry needs to be protected until the labor force is trained, the production techniques ate mastered and the operation becomes large enough to enjoy the economies of scale and to be able to compete in the market.

4. Yet it is no simple job to convert one currency into another without a loss while almost all currencies float every minute.

5. There are two major cultural issues that contribute to the success of international trade, the first aspect is language, including terms of transaction, and the other aspect is customs and manners.

IV. Translate the following sentences into English with the words given.

1. 这些因素的差别使一些国家得以种植某些作物而使另外一些国家只能选择进口他们消费的农产品。(enables...to...)

2. 这就产生了发展国际贸易的需要。(give rise to...)

3. 实际上,只有5%的人口从事农业生产并且他们主要种植水果和花卉。(be engaged in)

4. 尽管所有国家都能从国际贸易中获益,但在贸易方面各种不同的限制很普遍。(various kinds of)

5. 许多国家想发展多元化经济以减少经济上和政治上对外国的依赖。(be less dependent on)

Chapter 2

The Goals and Instruments of International Trade Policy

Pre-reading questions:
1. Do you have any idea about what a trade policy is?
2. What do you think "protectionism" is?
3. What trade policies has China adopted?
4. Are free trade policies the best for each nation in the world?
5. What instruments call be used to realize the goals of the international trade policy?

Text

Introduction

International trade is economic intercourse activity between countries, and is an important component of our national economy. International trade policy is general term for a variety of promotion and restrictive measures, which were taken to realize certain policy goals by the government. International trade policy is determined under the guidance of certain policy goals. Therefore, international trade policy is established and adjusted according to the goals of international trade policy. In order to achieve policy goals, it is necessary to take a variety of instruments, which include Tariff Barrier, Non-Tariff Barriers, Exchange Rate Measures, Revenue Measures and Pushing Exports.

International Trade Policy

International trade policy is a series of principles, laws and regulations, decrees, ordinances and so on, which are laid down by various countries in a given period of time to guide foreign trade activities according to their own politics, economy, military affairs, science and technology, etc.

The Goals of International Trade Policy

In general, a country's international trade policy services for its own interests. Specifically speaking, the goals of international trade policy mainly shows in the following aspects:

1. To protect the domestic markets

A country takes trade protection measures such as customs collection to limit the import of foreign goods so that the domestic markets serve for its own productions to protect its industrial developments, especially to protect the developments of its own infant industries that lack of competitiveness in order to improve their international competitiveness.

2. To expand the export markets of its own productions

Expansion of international market share is a main objective of international trade policy. A country reduces export cost and then improve the competitiveness of its own productions in the international markets through such trade measures as export subsidy, export credit and guarantee of export credits which provided by export-oriented departments and enterprises.

3. To accumulate capital and fund

Encouraging export will contribute to increasing foreign exchange earnings. Foreign exchange reserves is an important index of measuring a country's economy strength. Consequently, all countries promote the development of foreign trade positively by multiple channels to increase and diversify foreign exchange reserve.

4. To maintain its own political and economic security and stability

A country takes international trade policy to develop the international economic and technical cooperation so as to promote its own economic development. The development of foreign trade contributes to the improvement of a country's international status. Great economic strength will maintain country's political and economic security and stability.

5. To promote the economic development

Today the non-industrial countries of Asia, Africa, and Latin America are striving to accelerate their economic growth and to raise the living standard of the peoples. The pressing concern of these nations with the mammoth problem of economic development has led their government to regard international trade as all instrument to achieve such development to the exclusion of other ends. Thus, tariffs and other restrictive devices are employed to protect "infant industries" or to keep out "nonessential" consumer goods. On the other hand, capital goods and other "essential" imports are encouraged by subsidies or favorable exchange quotas. Exports may also be regulated in an attempt to promote economic development. Aside from these direct measures of control, economic development programs are likely to provoke disequilibrium in the balance of payments because of their inflationary impact on domestic income and price levels. Further controls may then be imposed to suppress the disequilibrium.

6. To achieve equilibrium of balance of payments

In the decade following World War II, the elimination of the dollar shortage occupied first place among the foreign economic policy objectives of Western European countries. In the 1960s and again in the 1980s, the U.S. balance of payments problem overshadowed other foreign economic issues. As we shall observe, balance of payments policy may conflict with domestic policies of full employment and non-inflationary growth. Sooner or later, all nations are compelled to remedy deficits in their balance of payments whether through market adjustments or controls. When a nation's reserves are low and its balance of payments is weak, the objective of payments equilibrium may come to dominate other objectives of its foreign economic policy and even of its domestic policy.

The Forms of International Trade Policy

Between the two extremes— autarky, which would regulate foreign trade out of existence, and free trade, which would impose no restrictions on whatsoever—there are many goals that serve to motivate foreign economic policy. Chief among them is protectionism—the protection of domestic producers against the free competition of imports by regulating their volume through tariffs, quotas and the like. Identification of a specific foreign economic policy as protectionist is sometimes difficult, since any policy that restricts imports has protectionist effects regardless of its objective.

Protectionism, therefore, has many guises and it shows a remarkable ability to adjust to new circumstances by employing arguments and stratagems suited to the times. In the 1980s, protectionism became a stronger influence on the foreign economic policies of the industrialized countries.

1. Protectionism

Protectionism is normally considered to cover all kinds of the government policies that favor domestic products over imported goods. It is regarded as the contrary of Manchesterism. There are many various measures of protectionism existing in the development of international trade. These measures involve not only the importing restrictions, such as tariff barriers and non-tariff barriers, but also exporting promotions.

2. Autarky

One extreme is the objective of autarky or natural self-sufficiency. A full autarky policy aims to rid the nation of all dependence on international trade and investment because this dependence is feared for the continuance of economic relations with other nations; the political counterpart of autarky is isolationism. Of course, most nations do not possess the domestic resources required to practice any significant degree of autarky. More common is a qualified autarky policy that seeks self-sufficiency in only certain articles of trade, generally of a strategic military value.

3. Manchesterism

Manchesterism is defined as a term designating the extreme form of the liberalist capitalism found particularly in the first half of the 19th century, taking its name from the city of Manchester (with its then flourishing textile industry); it propagates the free economy without any state control and with a total disregard for the social questions. It essentially means free working of the market forces in domestic and international markets. When the market forces could work freely in international market, it is free trade that would be achieved.

The controversy between Manchesterism and protectionism has been a continuing issue in most countries' trade policy. It seems that Protectionism is condemned severely while frequently applied by some countries.

Maybe, it is difficult to say which policy is better. Nations choose trade policy according to their national interests, not the term of Manchesterism or Protectionism.

The Instruments of International Trade Policy

International trade policy involves instruments as well as goals. In accordance with our decision to use a narrower interpretation of the scope of international trade policy, we shall take policy instruments to signify the tools (market variables, such as exchange rates, and direct controls) that are employed by governments with the intent to influence the magnitude, composition, or direction of international trade and factor movements.

1. Balance of payments policy

Balance of payments policy embraces all of the actions of government to maintain or restore equilibrium in their external accounts. In the face of an enduring, fundamental disequilibrium, governments generally respond to a deficit by deflating the domestic economy with monetary and fiscal instruments, devaluing the exchange rate, or imposing exchange controls over some or all international transactions. These basic instruments of adjustment may be used singly or in combination, and at times they may be rejected by governments in favor of policy instruments, such as tariffs and quantitative import restrictions, which are normally associated with other policy areas.

According to the law of comparative advantage, world resources can be most effectively used through specialization and trade. Full specialization is only possible when completely free trade is permitted. Unfortunately, every country in the world has trade barriers which are designed to protect its economy against international market forces. These restrictions may be divided into tariff barriers and non-tariff barriers.

2. Tariff barriers

Tariff barriers are the most common forms of trade restrictions. Tariffs may be levied on commodities leaving an area (export duties) or on merchandise entering an area (import duties). Import duties are more common than export duties because most nations are anxious to expand exports and increase foreign exchange earnings. The purpose of a duty is to increase the price of goods to make domestic goods more competitive or to raise tax revenues for a government. Duties may also be used to punish exporters or countries for unfair trade practices.

3. Trade and Investment policies

Trade policy refers to all government actions that seek to alter current account transactions, especially trade in merchandise. Historically, the main instrument of trade policy has been the import tariff, but today non-tariff barriers and export promotion are often of equal or greater importance.

Investment policy covers government actions both with respect to international long-term lending and borrowing (portfolio investment) and with respect to the international movement of business enterprise, which involves not only capital but management and technology as well (direct investment). Ordinarily the government in investing nations restrict investment outflows only for balance of payments reasons; indeed, they may promote investment outflows via inducements of one sort or another. On the other hand, although the government of borrowing or host nations seldom deter inflows of portfolio investment, they frequently do so with certain forms of direct investment while at the same time encourage other forms. Because of the rapid development of multinational companies that produce and sell throughout the world, foreign investment policy has assumed a critical importance for both home and host countries.

4. Agreements and treaties

Much of the international trade policy of a nation is effected through agreements and treaties with other nations. For the most part, the legal fights that individuals and business enterprises enjoy in the foreign country are those spelled out in treaties and agreements previously negotiated by their own governments. Thus, international treaties and agreements determine the treatment to be accorded foreigners and foreign interests. Generally speaking, this treatment is either national or most-favored-nation treatment. Under national foreigners possess the same right as nationals. Most-favored-nation treatment is based on a different concept of equity; it means that a nation treats a second nation as favorably as it treats any third nation. The main purpose of most-favored nation treatment is to eliminate national discrimination. Its greatest application is in the field of tariffs and other measures of commercial policy.

Vocabulary

instrument *n.* 工具；手段
make clear and explicit by the discussion of concrete examples
diversity *n.* 多样性；差异
the condition of being different, unlikeness
fundamental *adj.* 基本的；根本的
being or involving basic facts or principles
identification *n.* 辨认；鉴定
the act of designating or identifying something
autarky *n.* 自给自足
economic independence from external sources
continuance *n.* 持续；继续
the act of continuing an activity without interruption
counterpart *n.* 副本；相似的人或物
a person or thing having the same function or characteristics as another
liberal *adj.* 自由主义的
favoring an economic theory of laissez—faire and self-regulating markets
espouse *v.* 支持；赞成
to give one's loyalty or support to (a cause, for example); adopt
impose *v.* 强加；征税
to establish or apply as compulsory; levy
restriction *n.* 限制；约束
something that restricts; a regulation or limitation
regulate *v.* 管制；管理
to control or direct according to rules, principles, or laws
tariff *n.* 关税；税则
a list or system of duties imposed by a government on imported or exported goods
restrain *v.* 抑制；制止

to hold back or keep in check; control

stratagem *n.* 计策;计谋

a clever, often underhand scheme for achieving an objective

contemporary *adj.* 当代的;同时代的

current; or belonging to the same time

sustain *v.* 维持;持续

to keep in existence; maintain

reap *v.* 收获;收割

to obtain or to harvest

an abstract or general idea inferred or derived from specific instances

qualified *adj.* 合格的;有资格的

meeting the proper standards and requirements

strategic *adj.* 战略的

relating to or concerned with strategy

remedy *n.* 补救;赔偿

a solution to a particular problem

adjustment *n.* 调整;调节

the act of adjusting or the state of being adjusted

dominate *v.* 支配;占优势

to enjoy a commanding, controlling position in

accelerate *v.* 加速;促进

to cause to develop or progress more quickly

device *n.* 方法;手段

a technique or means

reserve *n.* 储备;储藏量

an amount in a fund used to meet cash requirements, emergency expenditures, or future defined requirements

regard *v.* 看待;当作

to look upon or consider in a particular way

specialization *n.* 专业化

where individuals become expels in producing certain goods or services that are then exchanged

objective *n.* 目标;目的
the goal intended to be attained

seek *v.* 寻求;寻找
to try to get or reach

eliminate *v.* 消除;去除
to do away with

dominant *adj.* 占主导地位的;占优势的
exercising the most influence or control

prominent *adj.* 显著的;突出的
immediately noticeable; conspicuous

philosophy *n.* 哲学;基本原理
a belief (or system of beliefs) accepted as authoritative by some group or school

paramount *adj.* 极为重要的;主要的
of chief concern or importance

frustrate *v.* 挫败;使感到沮丧
to prevent from accomplishing a purpose or fulfilling a desire; thwart

originate *v.* 起源;发生
to bring into being; create; start

employ *v.* 使用;雇用
to put to use or service

conflict *n.* 冲突;抵触
a state of disharmony between incompatible or antithetical persons, ideas, or interests; a clash

disturbance *n.* 干扰;打扰
something that disturbs, or act of disturbing

compel *v.* 强迫;迫使
to force, drive, or constrain

equilibrium *n.* 均衡

a condition in which all acting influences are canceled by others, resulting in a stable, balanced, or unchanging system

overshadow *v.* 遮掩；使……失色

to make insignificant by comparison; dominate

provoke *n.* 引起

give rise to; evoke

pressing *adj.* 紧迫的

demanding immediate attention; urgent

mammoth *adj.* 巨大的

of enormous size; huge

subsidy *n.* 补贴；津贴

financial assistance given by one person or government to another

attempt *n.* 企图；努力

earnest and conscientious activity intended to do or accomplish something

impact *n.* 影响；冲击

the effect or influence of one thing on another

overriding *adj.* 最重要的；高于一切的

more important than anything else

oppose(to) *v.* 反对；对立

to be in contention or conflict with

instrument *n.* 手段；工具

a means by which something is done; an agency

suppress *v.* 抑制；止住

to curtail or prohibit the activities of

tension *n.* 紧张(状态)

hostility or a strained relationship between people or groups

interpretation *n.* 解释；阐明

a mental representation of the meaning or significance of something

magnitude *n.* 数量；大小

the property of relative size or extent

injection *n.* 加入；注入

the forceful insertion of a substance under pressure

consideration *n.* 考虑;考虑的事项

a factor to be considered in forming a judgment or decision

application *n.* 应用;运用

the act of putting something to a special use or purpose

involve *v.* 包括;涉及

include; engage as a participant; embroil

signify *n.* 表示;意味

denote; mean

variable *n.* 变量;变数

something that is likely to vary; something that is subject to variation

accord *v.* 给予

to grant, especially as being due or appropriate

discrimination *n.* 歧视;分别对待

unfair treatment of a person or group on the basis of prejudice

transaction *n.* 交易

something transacted, especially a business agreement or exchange

Key terms

protectionism	保护主义
manchesterism	自由贸易主义
capital investment	资本投资
inflation	通货膨胀
infant industry	幼稚产业
capital goods	资本货物
multinational company	跨国公司
national treatment	国民待遇
non-tariff barriers	非关税壁垒
balance of payment	国际收支

Chapter 2 The Goals and Instruments of International Trade Policy

most-favored-nation treatment	最惠国待遇
portfolio investment	证券投资
tariff barriers	关税壁垒
export subsidy	出口补贴
export credit	出口信贷
autarky	自给自足
guarantee of export credits	出口信贷担保
domestic products	国货
dependence on international trade	国际贸易依存度
capitalism	资本主义
national interests	国家利益
the non-industrial countries	非工业化国家
consumer goods	消费品
favorable exchange quotas	顺差额
price levels	价格水平
monetary and fiscal instruments	货币和财政手段
the exchange rate	汇率
specialization	专业化分工
foreign exchange earnings	外汇收入
long-term lending and borrowing	长期信贷
investing nations	投资国
host nations	东道国
direct investment	直接投资

Post-Reading Activities

I. Answer the following questions based on what you have read in the text.

1. What is meant by the autarky policy in foreign trade?
2. What is protectionism?

3. What are the possible objectives in formulating an international trade policy?

4. Should economic development be the top priority for developing countries in formulating their foreign trade policies?

5. In what way do international trade and capital investment influence the employment situation of an economy?

6. What are the specific measures that can be taken under these policy instruments?

7. What are the foreign trade policy instruments mentioned in the article?

II. Look at the terms in the left-hand column and find the correct definitions in the right-hand column. Copy the corresponding letters in the blanks.

1. _____ portfolio investment   A. condition in which the value of a nation's imports is greater than its exports

2. _____ autarky   B. a policy of protecting domestic industries from foreign-made competition

3. _____ capital investment   C. the money paid to purchase a capital asset or a fixed asset

4. _____ balance of payment   D. a decline in the general price level of goods and services that results in increased purchasing power of money

5. _____ economic growth   E. the proportion of the total number of employed persons to the total number of persons in the labor force

6. _____ current account   F. the price of one currency stated in terms of anothercurrency

7. _____ exchange control   G. a policy of complete economic self-reliance-no trade or investment activities with the rest of the world

8. _____ multinational company   H. a statement of a country's trade and financial transactions with the rest of the world over a period of time

9. _____ employment rate   I. crease in the actual value of all final goods and

services produced by an economy

10. _____ exchange rate 　J. a company whose principal assets are the securities it owns in companies that actually provide goods or services it owns in companies that actually provide goods or services

11. _____ foreign policy 　K. the concept that countries must afford foreign companies the same access and other benefits they do local domestic firms

12. _____ trade deficit 　L. the net balance of a country's international payment arising from exports and imports together with unilateral transfers

13. _____ foreign aid 　M. a company with operations and investments in many countries around the world

14. _____ national treatment 　N. assistance given by one nation to another in the form of money, products, or technological aid

15. _____ protectionism 　O. a relatively consistent course of conduct pursued by one country in its relationship with another country

P. the purchase of foreign stocks, bonds or other securities

Q. the price of one currency stated in terms of another currency

R. a system of controlling inflows and out flows of foreign exchange

III. Fill in the blanks below with the most appropriate terms from the box.

| shift　gain from　self-sufficient　as well as　available |

1. The justification of free trade is that it enables a nation to _____ international specialization.

2. The domestic consumers benefit from international trade because it lowers the prices of goods and makes _____ goods that cannot be produced at home.

· 27 ·

3. The contribution of international trade is so immense that few countries could become _____ even with the greatest effort.

4. Every nation inhabits a global political and social environment _____ a global economic environment.

5. The composition of both U. S. imports and exports have _____ toward to manufactured high-tech products and away from industrial supplies and materials.

IV. Translate the following sentences into Chinese.

1. One of the goals of the import policy is directed at the acquisition of capital goods that embody the modern technology needed to develop China's economy.

2. Since implementation of reform and opening up policy, specially after its accession to the WTO, China has achieved remarkable growth in foreign trade.

3. A full autarky policy aims to rid the nation of all dependence on international trade and investment because this dependence is feared for the continuance of economic relations with other nations; the political counterpart of autarky is isolationism.

V. Translate the following sentences into English with the words given.

1. 经济学家一直在研究由于国际商务的扩展所引起的各种理论和实际问题。(engage in)

2. 很多经济学家认为,自由贸易能推动经济增长、提高生活水平。(argue)

3. 贸易保护主义表现形式多样,贸易保护主义通过在不同时期使用各种理由和计谋而具有超强的适应能力。(adjust)

Chapter 3

Modes of International Trade

> **Pre-reading questions:**
> 1. What does distribution refer to?
> 2. Do you know the meaning of sole distributor?
> 3. How many kinds do you know about agents?
> 4. What is consignment?
> 5. How many kinds do you know about auctions?

Text

Introduction

International trade modes refer to the common practices and channels between countries for the flow of commodities or services. With the fast development of international trade, trade modes tend to be increasingly diversified. This text's examination will be focused on the following methods of international sale of goods: Distribution; Agency; Consignment; Auction; Commodities futures transactions. On finishing this unit, the reader will have an understanding of modes of international trade.

Distribution or Sale

Distribution refers to a situation in which a distributor carries the products of one manufacturer and not those of the competing manufacturers. This may give the distributor the exclusive right to distribute the company's products in other territories.

By using this form, both parties (the manufacturer and the distributor) benefit from such exclusive arrangements. The manufacturer obtains more loyal and dependable outlets, and the distributor obtains a steady source of supply of special products and stronger seller support. Exclusive arrangements are legal as long as they do not substantially lessen competition or tend to create a monopoly and as long as both parties enter into the agreement on exclusive distribution voluntarily (according to the U.S. Clayton Act).

Distributors buy goods from the principals on their own account and take title to them and resell them to their customers in their territory. Thus, there is no contractual relationship between the principal and the ultimate customers. Instead there are separate sets of contracts: those between the principal and the distributor, and those between the distributor and the ultimate customers. The distributor takes his remuneration from the margin between the prices at which he buys the products and the prices at which he sells them to the customers. Since the distributor is an independent contractor, he assumes far more risks and obligations than an agent does: bad debts, advertising expenditure, warranty claims and maintenance, etc. Therefore, distributors generally enjoy more freedom and higher remuneration.

Two kinds of distributors are generally used:

● Sole or exclusive distributor

He is the only distributor in a territory.

● Non-exclusive distributor

There may be several non-exclusive distributors appointed by the principal or supplier in one territory.

General undertakings by the distributor

● To serve the principal diligently and faithfully during the continuance of the agreement in the territory

● Not to do anything that may prevent the sale or interfere with the development of sales of the products in the territory, such as dealing with competing goods

● To conform to all legislation rules and requirements existing in the territory

● Proper storage of the products

● Not to copy the products or any part of them for any other purpose

- To keep patent and trade mark notices
- Not to sell outside or export the product from the territory unless there is consent of the principal
- To provide the principal with sales report periodically

General undertakings by the principal

- To refer all inquiries received from the territory to the distributor
- To sell the products to the distributor with the lowest price charged at that time to any export customers of the principal
- To reserve the right to improve or modify the products with prior notice

Agency

Agency refers to a relationship between two parties, one, the principal, on whose behalf some action with a third party is being taken by the other, the other being the agent. Agency business in international trade means one party the owner of goods (the principal) entrusts the other the independent agent with the task of engaging in business activities in the name of the owner of the goods (the principal) and with his/her funds.

To establish an agency, there must be an agency agreement or contract signed between the principal and the agent, specifying their duties and rights. But before entering into such an agreement, the principal (normally a manufacturer) must be absolutely assured of the following four points:

- That he/she will be duly paid for his/her shipments
- That the importer/the agent has all the organization necessary to achieve the highest possible volume of sales
- That the importer/the agent is of such standing in his own markets as to command the respect and goodwill of the local buyers and consumers
- That the importer/the agent is unconnected with other business interests likely to hinder him/her from doing justice to his/her own products

An agent is a middleman who can act on behalf of a principal in specific matters. Many kinds of agents are active in international business nowadays, such as forwarding agents and clearing agents. What we will discuss here is selling agent. According to the power the principal has delegated to a selling agent, the agent may just introduce the potential customer to the principal or actually negotiates and concludes the contract between the two parties. They have the following characteristics:

An agent can only operate within the marketing territory authorized by the principal.

An agent does not carry stock. The goods are carried only as consignment inventory. Payment is based on delivery to the ultimate buyer.

The principal sets the retail price, retains title and controls the goods.

The profit and risk of loss remains with the principal, unless the agent is a del credere one.

Agents are usually paid by commission.

According to the scope of their authority, agents can be divided into several kinds:

1. Indenting agent

An indenting agent is the agent (exclusive or non-exclusive) appointed by a principal for marketing and promoting the products to potential customers within a territory. He needs to solicit inquiries for the products from potential customers in the territory. He will transmit them back to the principal who will then decide whether to accept the particular inquires, and upon what terms. Depending on the exact scope of his duties, the agent may or may not take part in the negotiation and conclusion of the contracts resulting from the inquiries.

2. Factor

A factor is appointed with the power to negotiate and conclude contracts in the territory on behalf of his principal. A factor may have a stock of the products, which will belong to the principal but will enable the factor to satisfy the contract that he negotiates.

3. Del credere agent

A del credere agent is the agent who takes responsibility for credit risks. If the buyer he introduces fails to pay the principal or breaks the contract, it is the agent's responsibility to cover the loss. Usually, del credere agents charge a higher commission.

4. Responsibilities of the agent and principal

Responsibilities of the agent

● To serve the principal as an agent on the terms of the agreement between them with all due and proper diligence, Maintain and provide necessary facilities at this own expense

- To pass all marketing information to the principal
- To comply with all laws and regulations in the territory
- To keep confidential to the principal, not disclose any useful information to any third party
- Not to act outside the territory

Responsibilities of the principal

- To supply to the agent free of charge a reasonable quantity of sales literature
- To supply necessary models or samples relating to the products
- Not submit offers nor effect sales in the territory without the agent's consent
- Responsibility to pay for the necessary expenses of the agent
- To pay commission to the agent in accordance with the agreement

Consignment

When using this method of selling, goods are sent by a principal (consignor) to an agent (consignee), usually in a foreign country for sale either at an agreed price or at the best market price.

The agent usually works for a commission, does not normally pay for the goods until they are sold and does not own them, although usually having possession of them. (That is why consignment is also looked on as one form of trade finance.)

The final settlement, often called a consignment account, details the cost of the goods, the expenses incurred, the agents commission, and the proceeds of the sale.

Under consignments, the consignor sends the goods to a foreign consignee who will sell the goods for the consignor according to the agreed terms. The essence of consignment trading is that goods exported on the consignment remain the property to the exporter. Therefore, consignment exports are not really exports because the exporter retains title to the goods until the importer sells the goods to final customers or third parties. So, the exporter is not paid until the goods are sold in the overseas marketplace.

Usually, the overseas consignee is advised of the goods being sent to him by means of a pro forma invoice. This gives him some idea of the price the exporter hopes to realize when the goods are sold. Any expenses incurred, such as warehousing, insurance or selling expenses, are for the consignor's account. When goods are sold, the consignee will render a sales report which shows the gross proceeds, the expenses incurred and the consignee's commission etc.

Consignment is rarely used between independent exporters and importers. There is too much risk for the exporters because they are not paid until all goods are sold in the foreign market. This may turn out to be a long period of time. Also, if the goods do not sell well on the foreign market, the exporter may have to get the goods back at his expense or sell the goods on discount. Moreover, most exporters feel that when an importer has his or her money tied up in inventory, he or she will make a greater sales effort. However, importers like consignment because it reduces their risk and requires no additional working capital.

Nonetheless, when the exporter wants to introduce goods to a foreign market, a consignment arrangement might be necessary to encourage the importer to handle the new merchandise. Furthermore, if the exporter wishes to control the foreign market price of his product, he can do so under a consignment contract.

Auction

Auction is another commonly used method of sale, in which goods are sold in public to the highest bidder.

International auctions are often used in developed countries for any property for which there are likely to be a number of competing buyers, such as houses, second-hand antique furniture, works of art, etc, as well as for certain commodities, such as tea, bristles, wool, furs, timber, etc, which must be sold as individual lots, rather than on the basis of standard sample or grading procedure. In most auctions, the goods to be sold are available for viewing before the sale and it is usual for the seller to put a reserve price on the articles offered, i.e. the articles are withdrawn from sale unless more than a specified price is bid.

In an auction, the auctioneer acts as agent for the seller in most cases and receives a commission on the sale price, An auctioneer is an agent of the seller, who must have the authority of the seller to sell, and must know of no defect in the seller's title to goods, without promising that a buyer will receive good title for a specific object. An advertisement that an auction will be held does not bind the auctioneer to hold it. It is illegal for a dealer (who buys at auction for subsequent resale) to offer a person a reward not to bid at auction.

Auctions are of two kinds: price-increasing auction and price-decreasing auction. Price-increasing auction is a kind of auction sale in which the auctioneer starts by calling a very low price predetermined and then let the bidders bid their prices until the highest bid is received by the auctioneer who indicates such receipt by bringing down the hammer. At the moment when the hammer is brought down, it means the deal is closed and he article is sold to the person making the highest bid. The other type of auction is known as price-decreasing auction or Dutch auction in which the auctioneer starts by calling a very high price and then reduces it gradually until a bid is received.

Commodities Futures Transactions

A futures transaction is the natural result of the high development of commodity exchange. In the past decade or so, commodity futures transaction has shown very quick growth.

Commodity futures transactions actually mean contracts for sale and delivery of a fixed quantity of a particular commodity at a fixed date in the future at a fixed price, made with the expectation that no commodity will be received immediately.

Commodities sold by using this method of sale are often wheat, soybeans, hogs, coffee, foodstuffs, metals, lumber, sugar, cocoa, crude oil, etc. In Japan, the U.S., the U.K, and other developed countries' big cities these are commodity exchanges or futures transaction centers for trading in those items.

Vocabulary

diversified *adj.* 多样化的,不同种类的
having variety of character or form or components; or having increased variety
examination *n.* 探讨
competing *adj.* 对抗的,竞争的
being in competition
consignment *n.* 寄售
the delivery of goods for sale or disposal
auction *n.* 拍卖
carry *v.* 经营,出售
distributor *n.* 经销商,分销商
territory *n.* 领地,领域,范围,经营范围

the geographical area under the jurisdiction of a sovereign state
obtain *vt.* 获得,得到
come into possession of
loyal *adj.* 忠诚的,忠心的;忠贞的
steadfast in allegiance or duty
dependable *adj.* 可信赖的,可靠的
worthy of being depended on or trust
outlet *n.* 专营店,经销店,销路,批发商店
steady *adj.* 稳定的,不变的
not subject to change or variation especially in behavior
substantially *adv.* 非常,大大地;基本上,大体上,总的来说
to a great extent or degree
lessen *vi.* 变少,减少;贬低
decrease in size, extent, or range
monopoly *n.* 垄断,专营服务
(economics) a market in which there are many buyers but only one seller
voluntarily *adv.* 志愿地;自动地,自发地
out of your own free will
principal *n.* 委托人
ultimate *adj.* 最后的;极限的;首要的;最大的
furthest or highest in degree or order; utmost or extreme
separate *adj.* 独立的,分开的
independent; not united or joint
remuneration *n.* 酬报;偿还;酬金
the act of paying for goods or services or to recompense for losses
assume *vt.* 取得(权力);承担,担任
take to be the case or to be true; accept without verification or proof
warranty *n.* 保证,担保
a written assurance that some product or service will be provided or will meet certain specifications

claim *n.* 索赔
diligently *adv.* 勤勉地,勤奋地
with diligence; in a diligent manner
continuance *n.* 继续,连续,持续的时间
the act of continuing an activity without interruption
interfere *vi.* 干预,干涉;调停,排解
conform *v.* 遵守
legislation *n.* 法律,法规
inventory *n.* 存货清单;财产目录
a detailed list of all the items in stock
negotiate *vi.* 谈判,协商,交涉
solicit *vt. & vi.* 恳求;征求;提起
make a solicitation or entreaty for something; request urgently or persistently
transmit *vt.* 传输;传送
entrust *v.* 委托,交托,托付
duly *adv.* 及时地,充分地
hinder *vt. & vi.* 阻碍,妨碍,阻挡
commission *n.* 佣金
essence *n.* 本质,实质;精华
the choicest or most essential or most vital part of some idea or experience
property *n.* 特性,属性;财产,地产
render *v.* 提出,开出;给予补偿
give or supply; give an interpretation or rendition of
discount *vi.* 折扣;贴现率;贴现
bidder *n.* 出价者,投标者
someone who makes a bid at cards
bristle 短而硬的毛发,鬃毛
reserve price (拍卖的)保留价格,最低价格
predetermined 预先决定的,事先安排的
log (尤指喂肥供食用的)猪
lumber 木材

Phrases

in the name of	为(某人),在……名下;凭……的权威,代表;以……的名义
do justice to	公平对待
competing manufacturer	竞争的经销商
volume of sales	销售量,销售额
final settlement	最终结算
consignment account	寄售账户
expenses incurred	开支
a particular commodity	某种特定的商品
for sb's account	由……支付
introduce goods	推销新产品

Key terms

exclusive distribution	包销
non-exclusive distribution	定销
agency	代理
consignment	寄售
auction	拍卖
distributor	分销商
exclusive right	独家代理权
monopoly	垄断
bad debt	呆账
the ultimate customers	最终消费者
middleman	中间人
delivery	交付
the retail price	零售价

Chapter 3 Modes of International Trade

authority	授权
indenting Agent	订购代理
factor	独立代理
consignor	寄售人
consignee	代销人
commission	佣金
bidder	竞买者
price-increasing auction	增价拍卖
price-decreasing auction	减价拍卖
forwarding agents	货运代理
clearing agents	清算代理
del credere agent	保付代理
commodities futures transactions	商品期货交易(也可用 commodity futures trading or dealings)
the U. S. Clayton Act	美国《克莱顿法》(a federal antitrust law prohibiting a range of business activities that may substantially lessen competition)
pro forma invoice	形式发票
working capital	流动资金;运营资金

Post-Reading Activities

I. Answer the following questions based on what you have read in the text.

1. How many kinds of trade forms are there in the text?
2. What is necessary to establish an agency?
3. Explain the two kinds of Auctions.
4. Which commodities are sold by using Commodities Futures Transactions?

II. Look at the terms in the left-hand column and find the correct definitions in the right-hand column. Copy the corresponding letters in the blanks.

1. _____ indenting agent

2. _____ Price-increasing auction

3. _____ Distribution

4. _____ Commodity futures transactions

5. _____ agency

6. _____ Consignment

A. the auctioneer starts by calling a very low price predetermined and then let the bidders bid their prices until the highest bid is received by the auctioneer who indicates such receipt by bringing down the hammer

B. contracts for sale and delivery of a fixed quantity of a particular commodity at a fixed date in the future at a fixed price, made with the expectation that no commodity will be received immediately

C. the agent (exclusive or non-exclusive) appointed by a principal for marketing and promoting the products to potential customers within a territory

D. the process of giving things out to several people, or spreading or supplying something

E. goods exported on the consignment remain the property to the exporter. Therefore, consignment exports are not really exports because the exporter retains title to the goods until the importer sells the goods to final customers or third parties

F. a business or an organization that provides a particular service, especially on behalf of other businesses or organizations

III. Translate the following sentences into Chinese.

1. Distributors buy goods from the principals on their own account and take title to them and resell them to their customers in their territory. Thus, there is no contractual relationship between the principal and the ultimate customers.

2. To establish an agency, there must be an agency agreement or contract signed between the principal and the agent, specifying their duties and rights. But before entering into such and agreement, the principal (normally a manufacturer) must be absolutely assured of the four points.

3. Consignment exports are not really exports because the exporter retains title to the goods until the importer sells the goods to final customers or third parties. So, the exporter is not paid until the goods are sold in the overseas marketplace.

4. When the exporter wants to introduce goods to a foreign market, a consignment arrangement might be necessary to encourage the importer to handle the new merchandise.

5. Commodities sold by using this method of sale are often wheat, soybeans, hogs, coffee, foodstuffs, metals, lumber, sugar, cocoa, crude oil, etc. In Japan, the U. S., the U. K, and other developed countries' big cities these are commodity exchanges or futures transaction centers for trading in those items.

IV. Translate the following sentences into English with the words given.

1. 代理人手中的存货均为寄售货物,待最终的买主付款后,委托人才能收到货款。(delivery)

2. 经销商利用买入价与卖出价赚取自己的利润。(prices at buys the products; sells them to the customers)

3. 销售最根本的特点就是出口产品仍为出口人所有。(remain to)

4. 出口商所冒的风险太大,因为他们必须等所有货物在国外市场上销售后才能得到货款,这可能会是相当长的时间。(turn out to be)

5. 签订此合同的当事人就预料不会立即获得商品。(expectation)

Chapter 4

International Trade in Services

Pre-reading questions:
1. Do you have an idea about international trade in services?
2. What services do you receive in your daily life?
3. How are services different from products?
4. Do you have any idea about GATS?
5. What do you think of the future of international trade in services?

Text

Introduction

International trade in services worldwide expanded rapidly in the late twentieth century, growing on average much faster than both the world GDP and world merchandise trade. In current U. S. dollars, total exports of services more than quadrupled between 1980 and 2002, from approximately $400 billion to about $1 600 billion.

When we talk about "trade" in services, it is not just trade in the conventional sense — where a product is produced in one country and sold to consumers in another country — but we mean the whole range of international transactions, including foreign investment and international movement of people, as consumers or providers of services. Thus, services "trade" encompasses: cross border trade in road and air transport; consumption by foreigners of tourism services; foreign direct investment in banking, communication, and distribution; and the temporary migration of doctors,

Chapter 4 International Trade in Services

teachers, and construction workers. Put this way, it is obvious that trade in services matters not just for the state of the services sector but for overall economic performance.

Definition of the International Trade in Services

What is meant by the term "international trade in services"? There is not even a consensus on the definition of what a service is. There is basic agreement about a number of characteristics of services. To start with, it is generally assumed that, unlike goods, services are not physically tangible. This quality is illustrated by the pragmatic description from the economist, according to which a service is "anything sold in trade that could not be dropped on your foot". In addition, services are usually regarded as being invisible, un-storable and un-transportable. They are mostly produced and consumed simultaneously. Goods, in contrast, are physically tangible, visible and storable, and do not need any direct interaction between producer and consumer. However, these pragmatic descriptions fail to describe the many peculiarities of the various service sectors or to provide a generally valid definition. Some services, for example, are certainly physical, tangible, storable and transportable, e. g. films, software programs, recorded music or blueprints. Some are visible, e. g. films and television programs, or do not require any direct interaction between producer and consumer, e. g. the services provided via telecommunications by banks, insurance companies or tourism firms. In addition, the technological advances in the communication and information sector are continually changing the situation.

So, according to the characteristics of services, services can be defined as economic output of intangible commodities that may be produced, transferred and consumed at the same time. However, services cover a heterogeneous range of intangible products and activities that are difficult to capture within a single definition and are sometimes hard to separate from goods. Services are outputs produced to order, and they typically include changes in the condition of the consumers realized through the activities of the producers at the demand of customers. Ownership over services cannot be established. By the time production of a service is completed, it must have been provided to a consumer. Examples of services are wholesale, hotel, catering, transport, insurance, education, property rental, telecommunications, marketing, health, and cultural and recreational services.

International trade in services is conventionally seen as trade in services between residents and non-residents of an economy. Since services require an immediate relationship between suppliers and consumers and in many cases are non-transportable, either the customer must go to the supplier or vice versa (for example, to get a haircut). International trade agreements concerning services often include provisions for suppliers' moving to the country of consumers. In such cases the traditional definition of "residents" and "non-residents" of an economy may not cover some important aspects of the international trade, such as services provided by foreign affiliates established abroad, many of which are considered "residents". The Manual on Statistics of International Trade in Services (2002) extends the scope of international trade in services to include foreign affiliates' trade in services and trade resulting from movement of natural persons. It is not suggested that these extensions be regarded as exports or imports.

GATS

Until 1995, no multilateral agreement existed on rules for the trade in services. This was largely due to a lack of knowledge about the services trade itself. However, the initiatives taken by certain private-sector groups in the developed world successfully led their governments to insist on the inclusion of international services in the Uruguay Round of negotiations which ultimately resulted into the General Agreement on Trade in Services (GATS) of the WTO (World Trade Organization).

The GATS is the first multilateral and legally enforceable agreement on trade and investment in the services sector. At the same time, it provides a framework for future negotiations to be held regularly on the further reduction of barriers to trade. It is an inter-governmental agreement to establish a multilateral framework of principles and rules for trade in services. The principal aim is the expansion of services trade under conditions of transparency and progressive liberalization and as a means of promoting the economic growth of all trading partners and the development of developing countries. The GATS covers almost all commercially traded services in any services sector except those supplied in the exercise of governmental authority. It addresses both services and service suppliers.

In order to achieve a pragmatic solution to the definition issue, the WTO Secretariat has drawn up a list of the service sectors covered by the GATS. Whilst it is neither binding nor final, it is used by most of the WTO countries. The list contains 12 major service sectors which are in turn subdivided into numerous subsections: business services; communication services; construction and other engineering services; distribution services (trade); educational services; environmental services; financial services; health-related and social services; tourism and travel-related services;

recreational, cultural and sporting services; transport services; other services not elsewhere included.

The GATS categorizes services according to the way in which they are provided. Four modes of delivery are laid down: cross border supply, consumption abroad, commercial presence, and movement of natural persons. The details are as follows:

Mode 1: Cross border supply. This mode covers as delivery of a service from the territory of one country into the territory of other country; examples are transportation services or internet-based trade.

Mode 2: Consumption abroad. This mode covers supply of a service of one country to the service consumer of any other country; examples are tourism or education overseas.

Mode 3: Commercial presence. This mode covers services provided by a service supplier of one country in the territory of any other country, examples are services rendered by foreign-owned banks.

Mode 4: movement of natural person. This mode covers services provided by a service supplier of one country through the presence of natural persons in the territory of any other country; examples include services provided by an on-site engineer.

The Factors Determining International Trade in Services

The strong expansion in international trade in services is being driven by the world-wide trend towards economic tertiarization. The improved availability of services and the rising demand for them are encouraging many suppliers to develop new markets abroad. What factors determine the position of a country and its suppliers in the international services trade? The main aspects are presented in this section:

It is now generally understood that the concept of "comparative advantage", which was originally developed for trade in goods, also applies in principle to international trade in services. This theory, which was developed by economist David Ricardo, says that a country engaged in international trade has competitive advantages in terms of those goods or services that require a relatively high input of production factors which are relatively abundant and thus cheap in that country. In contrast, a country will have competitive disadvantages in the case of those goods or services which require a high input of relatively scarce and therefore expensive production factors. A capital-rich country with high wages should therefore normally export goods and services which require a high input of capital. On the other hand, it should import goods and services which require a relatively high input of low-cost labour.

Competitiveness in international trade in services is primarily determined by structural factors which — as with trade in goods — vary from one country to another. It is generally assumed that the gap between the volume of trade in services and trade in goods is caused by the fact that services markets are more restricted than goods markets as a result of structural access barriers.

The main structural competitive factors are the availability of natural and human resources (human capital) in a country, e. g. the climate or natural beauty of the preferred tourist destinations, the size of the sales markets and the population, geographical proximity to the sales markets, or the vocational training, skills and motivation (the "services mentality" of the providers). The Netherlands, for example, serves as a transit country for maritime and air transport for large parts of Europe and has been able to build up a very powerful transport sector. Half of all imports into the E. U. enter via the Netherlands.

The natural ability to speak the leading world languages is a major competitive advantage in international trade in services. This partly explains America's competitive edge on the software market and the Internet, where 80% of the information comes in English.

In technology-intensive and capital-intensive services sectors like transport and communications, an important role is played by the availability of the necessary technical infrastructure and financial resources. Some of these factors exist "naturally" and can scarcely be influenced by government, whilst others can be altered by appropriate policies or business strategies. The latter applies, for example, to bringing policies on education and vocational training into line with the demands made by the international trade in services.

On the supply side, market access for foreign service providers is primarily dependent on the practical possibilities and the costs involved in overcoming the distance between suppliers and customers. Services which require direct contacts between suppliers and consumers often encounter structural market access barriers in international trade.

This in turn has widened the geographical areas and time horizons within which services are bought and sold, as can be seen from the expansion of large regional, national or international companies offering financial, air transport, telecommunications, hotel, fast food or car hire services. Financial services and securities trading, which were previously restricted to the opening hours of the national stock exchanges, are now available round the clock all around the world.

Another well-known example is provided by data processing and software services, which are provided in India for industrial and services companies world-wide.

It also makes sense to purchase foreign services when these relate to international transactions. Examples of this are export financing, transport insurance, reinsurance, the establishment of a communications centre for a globally operating company, etc.

A further reason for the internationalization of trade in services is the exploitation of commercial economies of scope and scale.

Companies derive economies of scope from the opportunity to serve many international markets and to utilize competitive advantages over national rivals. This usually involves a strategy of expansion with the establishment of an international network of branches. The main advantages are the global integration of information, data and marketing, the tying of internationally mobile clients to the company, and the cutting of investment and operating costs. However, these economies of scope do not exist for all service sectors, e. g. locally-based craft companies, local transport, or many regionally based professional services and small corporate structures. At one level, economies of scale can arise for the countries participating in world trade. If countries specialize in certain products and engage in trade with one another, they can take advantage of economies of scale in production. That is one of the reasons why small countries are often more intensively engaged in foreign trade than countries with large economic areas. By doing so, they overcome the difficulties of small sales markets.

Finally, "external" economies of scale arise when in-house production experience is disseminated (e. g. by outsourcing) across an entire sector or when production-related services are offered as an input for various industrial users, as happens in the computer industry in Silicon Valley.

On the demand side, the main structural impediments to the globalization of markets are specific regional needs and consumption patterns. These include historically and culturally determined consumer wishes, and especially differences of language.

In addition to the structural market access conditions, the relative competitive advantages and disadvantages of the service providers and their products—like price, quality, reliability, customer orientation, specialization, etc. — determine a country's position in the international trade in services. To this extent, there are no fundamental differences from merchandise trade.

The Future of International Trade in Services

The prospects for economic growth in the OECD countries are more positive than they have been for a decade. The developing countries and the countries in transition to the market economy also have a good growth outlook. Brazil, China, India, Indonesia and Russia are developing into major players in the world economy and in world trade. The traditional "industrial countries" and the new players are intensifying the international division of labour. This promotes economic development and trade. The process is also fostered by the liberalization of world trade. As a result of the Uruguay Round, the GATT Secretariat has forecast growth in world exports of goods up to 2005 of between 9% and 24% (depending on the underlying assumptions) and an annual increase in world output of between U.S. $ 110 and 315 billion — compared with the scenario without liberalization. Against this background, the prospects for further expansion in international trade in services can be assessed positively. It has been the fastest growing sector of world trade for years — albeit starting from a comparatively low level. This trend is likely to hold. The structural change towards the services and information society is continuing. In future periods of upswing, jobs will probably tend to be created in the tertiary sector rather than in industry. The export intensity of the services sector around the world is less than that of goods output, and there is scope for further development. In parallel to this, international direct investment is also expected to continue to grow appreciably.

The previous rapid growth in international trade in services has generally taken place — apart from in the single European market and other regional zones of integration and free trade — without a comprehensive liberalization of government market regulation. The multilateral process of liberalization in the WTO context, effective from 1995, will stimulate further growth. It will be supplemented and reinforced by agreements on liberalization like the result of the telecoms talks from February 1997 and the conclusion of the negotiations on financial services achieved at the end of 1997.

The actual impact on international trade will depend on strict adherence to the agreements made and on the extent to which businesses take advantage of the improved environment and global market liberalization. Notwithstanding all the positive expectations regarding the likely development of trade in services, the services sector will also have to face up to tougher competition, more aggressive methods of market development, and possibly new trade conflicts, both on the domestic and the world markets.

Vocabulary

merchandise *n.* 商品,货品
goods that are bought or sold; goods that are for sale in a shop/store

transaction *n.* 交易,业务,买卖
a piece of business that is done between people, especially an act of buying or selling

encompass *v.* 包含,涉及
to include a large number or range of things

tangible *adj.* 有形的
that can be clearly seen to exist

commodity *n.* (尤指国家间贸易的)商品,货物
a product or a raw material that can be bought and sold, especially between countries

heterogeneous *adj.* 各种各样的
consisting of many different kinds of people or things

affiliate *n.* 附属机构,分公司
a company, an organization, etc. that is connected with or controlled by another larger one

multilateral *adj.* 多边的,多国的
in which three or more groups, nations, etc. take part

proximity *n.* (时间或空间)接近,邻近
the state of being near sb/sth in distance or time

maritime *adj.* 海运的,船舶的
connected with the sea or ships

infrastructure *n.* (国家或机构的)基础设施,基础建设
the basic systems and services that are necessary for a country or an organization to run smoothly, for example buildings, transport and water and power supplies

integration *n.* 结合,整合
the act or process of combining two or more things so that they work together

disseminate *v.* 散布
to spread information, knowledge, etc. so that it reaches many people

impediment *n.* 妨碍,阻碍,障碍
something that delays or stops the progress of sth.

foster *v.* 促进,助长
to encourage sth to develop

scenario *n.* 预测
a description of how things might happen in the future

upswing *n.* 上升,进步
a situation in which sth. improves or increases over a period of time

albeit *conj.* 尽管,虽然
although

Phrases

interms of	根据,按照
round the clock	昼夜不停
derive from	得自
make sense	有意义
in parallel to	与……同时

Key terms

services	服务
international trade in service	国际服务贸易
trade in service	服务贸易
Uruguay Round of negotiation	乌拉圭回合谈判
General Agreement on Trade in Services (GATS)	服务贸易总协定
WTO Secretariat	世界贸易组织秘书处
cross border supply	过境交付
consumption abroad	境外消费
commercial presence	商业存在

movement of natural person	自然人移动
comparative advantage	比较优势
export finance	出口融资
transport insurance	运输保险投保
outsource	外包
Organization for Economic Co-operation and Development (OECD)	经济合作与发展组织
General Agreement on Tariffs and Trade (GATT)	关税及贸易总协定
free trade	自由贸易
market access	市场准入

Post-Reading Activities

I. Answer the following questions based on what you have read in the text.

1. What is the purpose of GATS?
2. What are the four modes of supply of the GATS?
3. How do structural factors determine international trade in services?
4. How do you understand the concept "comparative advantage"?

II. Look at the terms in the left-hand column and find the correct definitions in the right-hand column. Copy the corresponding letters in the blanks.

1. _____ wholesale services   A. the conditions, tariff and non-tariff measures, agreed by members for the entry of specific goods into their markets

2. _____ intangible   B. services involving selling goods (esp. in large quantities) to shopkeepers for resale to the public

3. _____ market access   C. services including goods and services acquired from an economy by travelers during visits of less than one

year. Transportation of passengers is excluded, as are goods purchased by travelers for resale in any economy

4. _____ cross border supply   D. which is hidden or not material, but known to be real

5. _____ travel services   E. services providing means of refreshing or entertaining oneself after work

6. _____ entertainment services   F. the delivery of a service from the territory of one country into the territory of other country

7. _____ financial services   G. services consisting of financial intermediation and auxiliary services, except those involving life insurance and pension funds. These services are mainly related to banks, stock exchanges, factoring or credit card enterprises and similar companies

III. Translate the following sentences into Chinese.

1. Goods, in contrast, are physically tangible, visible and storable, and do not need any direct interaction between producer and consumer.

2. International trade in services is conventionally seen as trade in services between residents and non-residents of an economy.

3. The GATS is the first multilateral and legally enforceable agreement on trade and investment in the services sector.

4. Commercial presence covers services provided by a service supplier of one country in the territory of any other country.

5. Movement of natural person covers services provided by a service supplier of one country through the presence of natural persons in the territory of any other country.

IV. Translate the following sentences into English with the words given.

1. 境外消费，即在一方境内向任何其他方的服务消费者提供服务。(consumption aboard)

2. 一国在生产产品或提供服务时所需大量投入的生产要素在其国内丰富而廉价，此时该

国便在该类产品或服务的国际贸易中便具有竞争优势。(in terms of)

3. 现在世界各地都可以昼夜不停地提供金融和证券交易服务。(round the clock)

4. 尽管起点相对较低,它仍已成为近年来世界贸易增长最快的部分。(albeit)

5. 与此同时,国际直接投资预计也将明显地继续增长。(in parallel to)

Chapter 5

Free Ports and Foreign-Trade Zones

Pre-reading questions:

1. Do you have an idea about Free Ports and Foreign-Trade Zones?
2. What is the function of Free Ports and Foreign-Trade Zones?
3. How can companies benefit from using Free Ports and Foreign-Trade Zones?
4. How much do you know about the GATT?

Text

Introduction

Foreign Trade Zone (FTZ)

A Free Trade Zone (FTZ) or export processing zone (EPZ), also called foreign-trade zone, formerly free port is an area within which goods may be landed, handled, manufactured or reconfigured, and reexported without the intervention of the customs authorities. Only when the goods are moved to consumers within the country in which the zone is located do they become subject to the prevailing customs duties.

Free Port

Free port, port, or section of a port, exempt from customs regulations. Goods may be landed at a free port for storage and handling, and they may even be processed into manufactured goods. Duty is charged only if the goods are moved from the free port into the adjacent territory.

Free-Trade Area (FTA)

Differentiating from the Free Trade Zone (FTZ), a Free-Trade Area (FTA) is a trade bloc whose member countries have signed a free-trade agreement (FTA), which eliminates tariffs, import quotas, and preferences on most (if not all) goods and services traded between them.

A Free Trade Agreement (FTA) is a legally binding agreement between two or more countries to reduce or eliminate barriers to trade, and facilitate the cross border movement of goods and services between the territories of the Parties.

Free Trade Zone (FTZ) and Free Port

A Free Trade Zone (FTZ) is a specified area within the territorial jurisdiction of a country where there is either a minimum or no customs control on entry or exit of goods.

A free port (FP) is characterized by its whole harbor plants (quays, wharves, warehouses, factories, etc.) that are considered by law outside the customs boundaries.

FTZ's and FP's are not subject to such standard government restrictions on trade such as customs treatment, banking laws, taxation, labour laws and economical laws and transactions.

The relation between the free transit of goods within FTZ's and FP's and the corresponding increase of counterfeiting activities in these areas has become one of the most important issues relating to the protection of trademark rights. Goods passing through FTZ's or FP's and transshipped through multiple ports, creates opportunities for counterfeiters to disguise the true country of origin of goods. Counterfeiters also take advantage of customs territories where border enforcement for transshipped or in transit goods is known to be weak, with the intention of passing the goods through those customs territories to their destination.

History of Free Trade Zone (FTZ) and Free Port

Free-trade zones are organized around major seaports, international airports, and national frontiers — areas with many geographic advantages for trade. It is a region where a group of countries has agreed to reduce or eliminate trade barriers. Free trade zones can be defined as labor intensive manufacturing centers that involve the import of raw materials or components and the export of factory products.

The world's first Free Trade Zone was established in Shannon, Co. Clare, Ireland Shannon Free

Zone. This was an attempt by the Irish Government to promote employment within a rural area, make use of a small regional airport and generate revenue for the Irish economy. It was hugely successful, and is still in operation today. The number of worldwide free-trade zones proliferated in the late 20th century. In the United States free-trade zones were first authorized in 1934.

Free ports originated in the late Middle Ages, when the burdensome tariffs charged by many petty states threatened the reemerging maritime commerce. The high tariffs later levied in the period of mercantilism necessitated additional free ports. In the 19th century, the danger of smuggling caused the closing of many free ports. In Europe, Copenhagen, Danzig, and Hamburg were free ports until 1939; in East Asia, Hong Kong and Singapore still are. In the United States, bonded warehouses serve some of the functions of the free port, permitting goods to be stored and processed in specially licensed warehouses if a bond exceeding the amount of the customs duties is first posted. In 1934 the Foreign Trade Zones Act authorized the establishment of free ports in the United States, but with a prohibition on manufacturing. The first American free port was opened in New York City in 1937, and others have since been added. Many international airports have free ports.

Free trade zones are developed in places that are geographically advantageous for trade. Places near international airports, seaports, and the like are preferred for developing free trade zones.

Free Trade Zone and Developing Countries

International Free Trade Zones are placed mostly in developing countries. The Free Trade Zone can be defined as a labor-intensive manufacturing hub, which involves the import of components and raw materials, and the produced goods are exported to different countries. It was in the initial decades of the 20th century that the Free Trade Zones in Latin America came into prominence. International FTZs are spread over 116 countries across the world. Among the major products that are produced in Free Trade Zones electronics goods, cloths, toys, and shoes are worth mentioning.

The setting up of Free trade zones have also been criticized, for encouraging commercial activities sometimes under the influence of corrupt governments, and for providing the multinational corporations with more economic liberty. A number of developing countries have allowed the local industrialist to set up units located within the free trade zones, in order to exploit the export-based incentives.

The governments of these countries provide relaxation of the rules pertaining to environmental protection and negligence to the workers, tax holiday for the first five years, and sometimes the initial cost of setting up of the production unit. The Free trade zones are located in the developing countries. Outsourcing the zone to the FTZ operator minimizes the bureaucracy and the businesses established in that zone may be given tax benefits.

Purpose of International Free Trade Zones

The main idea behind creation of Free Trade Zones is to facilitate cross-border trade by removing obstacles imposed by customs regulations. Free Trade Zones ensure faster turnaround of planes and ships by lowering custom related formalities. FTZs prove to be beneficial both for the importers and exporters, as these zones are designed to reduce labor cost and tax related expenditures. Free Trade Zones help the traders to utilize the available business opportunities in the best possible way. FTZs promote export-oriented industries. These zones also help to increase foreign exchange earnings. Employment opportunities created by free trade zones help to reduce unemployment problem in the less developed economies.

One of the main purposes of the free trade zones is to develop the economy of that location by providing more job opportunities, business options, manufacturing options, etc.

These zones are mostly used by transnational corporations for establishing factories for the manufacturing of several goods. The goods depend on the availability of the raw material, skilled labor, and well-equipped technical staff.

There were around 3 000 free trade zones across 116 countries in the year 1999, where nearly 43 million people were working. These FTZs produce various goods such as shoes, clothes, sneakers, toys, convenient foods items, electronic goods, etc. The other important purposes of such trade zones are the development of export-oriented units, increase in the foreign exchange earnings, and generation of employment opportunities.

The U.S. Foreign Trade Zone

Foreign Trade Zones (FTZs) were created in the United States to provide special customs procedures to U.S. plants engaged in international trade-related activities. Duty-free treatment is accorded items that are processed in FTZs and then reexported, and duty payment is deferred on items until they are brought out of the FTZ for sale in the U.S. market. This helps to offset customs advantages available to overseas producers who compete with domestic industry. The Foreign-Trade Zones (FTZ) Board (composed of representatives from the U.S. Departments of Commerce and Treasury) has its operational staff in the International Trade Administration's Import Administration.

How can companies benefit from using FTZs?

FTZs are considered to be outside of U.S. Customs Territory for the purpose of customs duty payment. Therefore, goods entering FTZs are not subject to customs tariffs until the goods leave the zone and are formally entered into U.S. Customs Territory. Merchandise that is shipped to foreign countries from FTZs is exempt from duty payments. This provision is especially useful to firms that import components in order to manufacture finished products for export.

There is no time limit on goods stored inside a FTZ and certain foreign and domestic merchandise held in FTZs may be exempted from state and local inventory taxes. This allows firms to minimize their costs while their products are waiting to be shipped. In addition, quota restrictions are in some cases waived for items entering an FTZ; however, the restrictions would apply if the items were to enter the U.S. market.

A variety of activities can be conducted in a zone, including assembling, packaging, destroying, storing, cleaning, exhibiting, re-packing, distributing, sorting, grading, testing, labeling, repairing, combining with foreign or domestic content, or processing. Manufacturing and processing require specific FTZ Board approval, however.

Can Foreign Trade Zones hurt domestic producers?

FTZ activity must not conflict with U.S. trade policy or harm domestic industry or other domestic plants outside of zones. The FTZ Board requires that zone manufacturing activity result in a significant public benefit and a net positive economic effect. In addition, the U.S. Customs Service supervises all zone activity and ensures that all customs and FTZ Board requirements are observed.

What are the different types of FTZs?

FTZs are divided into general-purpose zones and subzones. The Foreign-Trade Zones Board accepts and reviews applications for both. State or local governments, port authorities, nonprofit organizations, or economic development agencies typically sponsor general-purpose zones. General-purpose zones involve public facilities that can be used by more than one firm, and are most commonly ports or industrial parks used by small to medium sized businesses for warehousing/distribution and some processing/assembly. Subzones, on the other hand, are sponsored by general-purpose zones, but typically involve a single firm's site which is used for more extensive manufacturing/processing or warehousing/distribution that cannot easily be accomplished in a general-purpose zone.

The U. S. Foreign-Trade Zones Program

Today, the trade policy of the United States is based on a free trade model. This theoretical model recognizes only the economic beneficiaries of free trade; it acknowledges that the costs (or losers) resulting from free trade are negligible. In reality, however, free trade has benefits and costs. No doubt, the benefits far outweigh the costs; however, the costs are very real. The Foreign-Trade Zones program offers a way to mitigate the costs of free trade. In doing so, the program allows the United States economy to enjoy relatively greater benefits from its free trade initiatives. The various benefits offered by the Foreign-Trade Zones program make it an effective response to the problems that arise when the $8.5 trillion dollar U. S. economy operates within the rapidly changing international trade environment.

The U. S. Foreign-Trade Zones program was created by the Foreign-Trade Zones Act of 1934. The Foreign-Trade Zones Act was one of two key pieces of legislation passed in 1934 in an attempt to mitigate some of the destructive effects of the Smoot-Hawley Tariffs, which had been imposed in 1930. The Foreign-Trade Zones Act was created to "expedite and encourage foreign commerce" in the United States. This is accomplished through the designation of geographical areas, in or adjacent to Customs Ports of Entry, where commercial merchandise receives the same Customs treatment it would if it were outside the commerce of the United States. Merchandise of every description may be held in the Zone without being subject to Customs duties and other ad valorem taxes. This tariff and tax relief is designed to lower the costs of U. S. based operations engaged in international trade and thereby create and retain the employment and capital investment opportunities that result from those operations. These special geographic areas—Foreign-Trade Zones—are established "in or adjacent to" U. S. Ports of Entry and are under the supervision of the U. S. Customs Service. Since 1986, U. S. Customs' oversight of FTZ operations has been conducted on an audit-inspection basis, whereby compliance is assured through audits and spot checks under a surety bond, rather than through on-site supervision by Customs personnel.

The FTZ program has grown profoundly over the last 30 years. In 1970 there were 8 Foreign-Trade Zone projects (with a total of 3 Subzones) in the United States. Today there are over 230 Foreign-Trade Zone projects (with nearly 400 Subzones) in the United States. This growth is the result of changes in the FTZ program. These changes have caused the FTZ program to evolve into an important means by which U. S. based companies can enhance their cost-competitiveness, and as a means by which the United States can practice both the letter and the spirit of its trade laws.

From 1934 through and beyond the Second World War, Foreign-Trade Zones were used only on a very limited basis. The reason for this was clear: the prohibition against manufacturing activity. While Zones lay virtually dormant, the 16 years between 1934 and 1950 saw a complete change in the dynamics of trade — a change which would create the need for the FTZ program within the U. S. manufacturing sector.

The General Agreement on Tariffs and Trade (known by its acronym "GATT") became the working model by which more than 120 nations participated in round after round of multilateral tariff reductions for nearly 50 years. From 1946 until 1995, the GATT served to break down the barriers to trade on a worldwide basis. This expansion of trade played a critical part in the 50-year economic boom in member countries following the end of the Second World War.

Early in this period, an important amendment to the Foreign-Trade Zones Act was made. In 1950, those members of Congress who were the original champions of the Foreign-Trade Zones Act of 1934, convinced their colleagues of the wisdom of allowing manufacturing activity in Foreign-Trade Zones. Approval for manufacturing in Zones would be done on a case-by-case basis, and, as was the case in other FTZ's around the world at that time, goods manufactured in Zones would be assessed Customs duty based on their full value, including domestic parts, labor, overhead and profit, upon entry into domestic commerce. This was in keeping with the so-called "island" model of FTZs in which the activity conducted within each Zone is totally segregated from the domestic economy.

While this new amendment to the Foreign-Trade Zones Act advanced the cause of U. S. Foreign-Trade Zones significantly, it did little to spur Zone manufacturing activity. Since the U. S. tariff structure was still largely biased in favor of domestic production activity, firms who imported foreign parts to produce finished products for the domestic market were at a competitive advantage in relation to their foreign-based counterparts. Zone manufacturing for production devoted exclusively to export sales was a rare phenomenon. Thus, throughout the 1950's and 1960's the U. S. Foreign-Trade Zones program was of little practical utility to businesses. During this time period, round after round of GATT agreements were reached, and the competitive environment of global trade changed significantly. Many of the tariff barriers were reduced by the simple reduction in Customs duty rates on a multilateral basis. As trade negotiators completed these agreements, duty rates on a wide variety of products were lowered worldwide. This promoted international trade through freer market access and lead to its expansion. However, as round after round of global trade agreements were implemented, it became clearer to some that this freer market access came with an unexpected cost.

As befits most professional negotiators, the community of international trade negotiators shared (as, no doubt, it still does), the common characteristic of trying to gain the most for their native countries, while yielding the least. Naturally, over the course of time, high value-added manufactured goods would be the subject of intense trade negotiation. As agreements for tariff reductions on high value-added finished products proliferate, so do inconsistencies within the tariff structures of individual nations.

The classic, domestically-biased duty rate relationship between raw materials, parts and components which make up intermediate stages of production, and a given finished product, is characterized by increased rates of import duties as value is added in the production process. This classic structure meets the twin aims of tariffs: to raise revenue and encourage domestic production activities (which, in the United States are taxed through individual and corporate taxes).

However, as multilateral tariff agreements reduce duty rates on a world-wide basis, an odd set of duty rate relationships can sometimes occur as a result of a particular end product's reduced tariff rate. On occasion, the duty rate applicable to imported intermediate parts is higher, rather than lower, than the duty rate that applies to the finished product. While providing market access for the end product—a desired result because of a corresponding concession by other member nations—this duty rate relationship also imposes an unintended counterproductive cost on the domestic producer of that end product. Now the domestic producer is competing with its foreign-based counterpart at an inherent cost disadvantage. Why? Because it must now pay a higher rate on one or more of its imported parts than its foreign-based competitor pays to import its finished product. This tariff imposition reduces the domestic producer's profit margin and thereby makes it irrational for it to continue to make the finished product domestically. Such duty rate relationships are known as irrational duty rate relationships or "inverted tariffs." Such a tariff structure is biased against the higher value-added activity to produce the finished product domestically. In this situation, value-added activity (which, if conducted domestically, would produce income taxes on profits and wages) is encouraged to be moved to a foreign location.

By 1980, the combination of cheap and efficient transportation, and the use of such programs as Mexico's Maquiladora, or "twin plant" program, provided the means for U.S. firms to shift production of their products overseas, and for foreign-based firms to more easily compete in the U.S. market. Falling tariff rates, and, in particular, the way they affected the U.S. tariff structure, provided additional motivation to conduct value-added activity overseas.

Fortunately, a truly effective remedy was at hand. Since 1972, the National Association of Foreign-Trade Zones (NAFTZ) has served the interests of the communities and companies who participate in the U.S. Foreign-Trade Zones program. The NAFTZ observed the existing Customs and tariff treatment afforded to domestic parts shipped overseas for value-added activity and then returned to theU.S.. The NAFTZ began to press for equivalent tariff treatment of products manufactured in a U.S. Foreign-Trade Zone environment. The NAFTZ asserted that Customs duty on products manufactured in Zones should not be assessed on U.S. value-added—that is, value which consists of domestic materials, parts, labor, overhead, or profit.

On April 12, 1980, the U.S. Customs Service issued a formal ruling that agreed with the NAFTZ's position. At last, the U.S. Foreign-Trade Zones program, born in 1934, could be of real utility in attracting and retaining U.S. based economic activity. This economic activity generates investment, labor, and profit, which collectively produce far more tax revenues than do Customs duties.

Now, at last, the U.S. based manufacturer could bring foreign-sourced parts or materials into the Zone, pay no duty, incorporate those parts or materials into a finished product using U.S. parts and labor, and, if the finished product entered the U.S. commerce, pay duty on the value of the foreign non-duty-paid content only. This "integrated" model, which has replaced the previous "island" model, has spurred the growth in the U.S. Foreign-Trade Zones program, and has allowed U.S. based manufacturers to engage in economical sourcing—from both foreign and domestic suppliers—to displace imports of foreign-produced finished products. This, along with the overall expansion of global trade, is why the number of Zone projects, and the number of Subzones, has grown so profoundly.

In historical summary, the 1950 amendment which allowed manufacturing, and the 1980 ruling which effectively eliminated the "island" model for U.S. Zones (thereby integrating Zone activity with the U.S. economy), provided the legal and regulatory framework for the Foreign-Trade Zones program to effectively serve U.S. based businesses. Round after round of multilateral trade agreements created the need for the U.S. government to make exceptions to the published tariff rates in instances where the structure of the U.S. tariff is counterproductive. Therefore, today, the Zones program acts as a tool by which the United States can practice both the letter and spirit of its trade laws and policies.

Chapter 5 Free Ports and Foreign-Trade Zones

Establishing a Foreign-Trade Zone

The Foreign-Trade Zones Act of 1934 created a Foreign-Trade Zones Board to review and approve applications to establish, operate, and maintain foreign-trade zones. The Board may approve any zone or subzone which it deems necessary to serve adequately "the public interest".

The Board also regulates the administration of foreign-trade zones and the rates charged by zone "grantees".

CBP must approve activation of the zone before any merchandise is admitted under the Foreign-Trade Zones Act.

It is the intent of the U. S. foreign-trade zone program to stimulate economic growth and development in the United States. In an expanding global marketplace there is increased competition among nations for jobs, industry and capital. The FTZ program was designed to promote American competitiveness by encouraging companies to maintain and expand their operations in the United States.

The FTZ program encourages U. S. based operations by removing certain disincentives associated with manufacturing in the United States. The duty on a product manufactured abroad and imported into the U. S. is assessed on the finished product rather than on its individual parts, materials, or components. The U. S. based manufacturer finds itself at a disadvantage compared with its foreign competitor when it must pay a higher rate on parts, materials, or components imported for use in a manufacturing process. The FTZ program corrects this imbalance by treating products made in the zone, for the purpose of tariff assessment, as if it were manufactured abroad. At the same time, this country benefits because the zone manufacturer uses U. S. labor, services, and inputs.

Role of CBP

CBP is responsible for the transfer of merchandise into and out of the FTZ and for matters involving the collection of revenue. The Office of Regulations and Rulings at CBP Headquarters provides legal interpretations of the applicable statute, CBP Regulations and procedures.

The Port Director of CBP, in whose port a zone is located, is charged with overseeing zone activity as the local representative of the Foreign-Trade Zones Board. He or she controls the admission of merchandise into the zone, the handling and disposition of merchandise in the zone, and the removal of merchandise from the zone. In addition to the Foreign-Trade Zones Act, he or

she enforces all laws normally enforced by CBP that are relevant to foreign-trade zones.

Zones are supervised by FTZ Coordinators through compliance reviews and visits; the security of the zone must meet certain requirements.

What may be placed in zones?

Any foreign or domestic merchandise not prohibited by law or other exception listed below, whether dutiable or not, may be taken into a foreign-trade zone.

Merchandise, which lawfully cannot be imported into the United States, is prohibited without exception. Furthermore, placing merchandise subject to a quota into a zone cannot circumvent quota on the imported merchandise.

On the other hand, merchandise for which a quota is filled or for which a quota on entry is established, may be placed into a zone until the quota opens or is removed since foreign-trade zones are considered outside CBP territory for entry purposes. Such products, with the exception of certain textiles, may be manipulated or manufactured while in the zone into a product not subject to quota.

Some Federal agencies regulate storage and handling in the United States of certain types of merchandise, such as explosives. Depending on the nature of the requirements and the particular characteristics of the zone facility, such merchandise may be excluded. Moreover, agencies, which license importers or issue importation permits may block admissions to a zone, which are not properly licensed or permitted.

The Foreign-Trade Zones Board may exclude from a zone any merchandise that is in its judgment detrimental to the public interest, health, or safety. The Board may place restrictions on certain types of merchandise, which would limit the zone status allowed, the kind of operation on the merchandise in a zone, the entry of the merchandise into the commerce, or similar transactions or activities.

What may be done in zones?

The Foreign-Trade Zones Board may exclude from a zone any merchandise that is in its judgment detrimental to the public interest, health, or safety. The Board may place restrictions on certain types of merchandise, which would limit the zone status allowed, the kind of operation on the merchandise in a zone, the entry of the merchandise into the commerce, or similar transactions or activities.

Many products subject to an internal revenue tax may not be manufactured in a zone. These products include alcoholic beverages, products containing alcoholic beverages except domestic denatures distilled spirits, perfumes containing alcohol, tobacco products, firearms, and sugar. In addition, the manufacture of clock and watch movements is not permitted in a zone.

No retail trade of foreign merchandise may be conducted in a FTZ. However, foreign and domestic merchandise may be stored, examined, sampled, and exhibited in a zone.

The Advantages of Using a Foreign-Trade Zone

CBP duty and federal excise tax, if applicable, are paid when the merchandise is transferred from the zone for consumption.

While in the zone, merchandise is not subject to U. S. duty or excise tax. Certain tangible personal property is generally exempt from state and local ad valorem taxes.

Goods may be exported from the zone free of duty and excise tax.

CBP security requirements provide protection against theft.

Merchandise may remain in a zone indefinitely, whether or not subject to duty.

The rate of duty and tax on the merchandise admitted to a zone may change as a result of operations conducted within the zone. Therefore, the zone user who plans to enter the merchandise for consumption to CBP territory may normally elect to pay either the duty rate applicable on the foreign material placed in the zone or the duty rate applicable on the finished article transferred from the zone whichever is to his advantage.

Merchandise imported under bond may be admitted to a FTZ for the purpose of satisfying a legal requirement of exporting the merchandise. For instance, merchandise may be admitted into a zone to satisfy any exportation requirement of the Tariff Act of 1930, or an exportation requirement of any other Federal law (and many state laws) insofar as the agency charged with its enforcement deems it so.

Criticism

Free trade zones are domestically criticized for encouraging businesses to set up operations under the influence of other governments, and for giving foreign corporations more economic liberty than is given indigenous employers who face large and sometimes insurmountable "regulatory" hurdles in developing nations. However, many countries are increasingly allowing local entrepreneurs to locate inside FTZs in order to access export-based incentives. Because the multinational corporation is able to choose between a wide range of underdeveloped or depressed nations in setting up overseas factories, and most of these countries do not have limited governments, bidding wars (or "races to the bottom") sometimes erupt between competing governments.

Sometimes the domestic government pays part of the initial cost of factory setup, loosens environmental protections and rules regarding negligence and the treatment of workers, and promises not to ask payment of taxes for the next few years. When the taxation-free years are over, the corporation that set up the factory without fully assuming its costs is often able to set up operations elsewhere for less expense than the taxes to be paid, giving it leverage to take the host government to the bargaining table with more demands, but parent companies in the United States are rarely held accountable.

Foreign-Trade Zones (FTZ) are secure areas under U. S. Customs and Border Protection (CBP) supervision that are generally considered outside CBP territory upon activation. Located in or near CBP ports of entry, they are the United States' version of what are known internationally as free-trade zones.

Authority for establishing these facilities is granted by the Foreign-Trade Zones Board under the Foreign-Trade Zones Act of 1934, as amended. The Foreign-Trade Zones Act is administered through two sets of regulations, the FTZ Regulations and CBP Regulations.

Foreign and domestic merchandise may be moved into zones for operations, not otherwise prohibited by law, including storage, exhibition, assembly, manufacturing, and processing. All zone activity is subject to public interest review. Foreign-trade zone sites are subject to the laws and regulations of the United States as well as those of the states and communities in which they are located.

Under zone procedures, the usual formal CBP entry procedures and payments of duties are not required on the foreign merchandise unless and until it enters CBP territory for domestic consumption, at which point the importer generally has the choice of paying duties at the rate of either the original foreign materials or the finished product. Domestic goods moved into the zone for export may be considered exported upon admission to the zone for purposes of excise tax rebates and drawback.

Qualified public or private corporations that may operate the facilities themselves or contract for the operation sponsors foreign-trade zones. The operations are conducted on a public utility basis, with published rates. A typical general-purpose zone provides leasable storage/distribution space to users in general warehouse-type buildings with access to various modes of transportation. Many zone projects include an industrial park site with lots on which zone users can construct their own facilities.

Subzones are normally private plant sites authorized by the Board and sponsored by a grantee for operations that usually cannot be accommodated within an existing general-purpose zone.

Vocabulary

amendment *n.* 修正案
formal revision of, addition to, or change, as in a bill or a constitution

assemble *vt.* 装配
to fit together the parts or pieces of

designation *n.* 指定
the act of designating; a marking or pointing out

disguise *vt.* 掩饰；隐瞒
to furnish with a disguise

disincentive *n.* 不利于经济发展的因素
something that prevents or discourages action; a deterrent

drawback *n.* 退税
a refund or remittance, such as a discount on duties or taxes for goods destined for reexport

duty *n.* [税收] 关税
a tax charged by a government, especially on imports

indigenous *adj.* 本土的
originating and growing or living in an area or environment

jurisdiction *n.* 管辖权
authority or control

reconfigure *vt.* 重新配置、组合
to rearrange the elements or settings of

revenue *n.* 收入
the income of a government from all sources appropriated for the payment of the public expenses

segregate *vt.* 使隔离；使分离

to separate or isolate from others or from a main body or group

tariff *n.* 关税

duties or a duty imposed by a government on imported or exported goods

detrimental *adj.* 不利的；有害的

leverage *n.* 杠杆作用

the action of a lever

levy *vt.* 征收（税等）

to impose or collect (a tax, for example)

Maquiladora *n.* 美墨联营工厂（位于墨西哥境内，属于美国公司）

an assembly plant in Mexico, especially one along the border between the United States and Mexico, to which foreign materials and parts are shipped and from which the finished product is returned to the original market

mercantilism *n.* 重商主义

the theory and system of political economy prevailing in Europe after the decline of feudalism, based on national policies of accumulating bullion, establishing colonies and a merchant marine, and developing industry and mining to attain a favorable balance of trade

mitigate *vi.* 减轻

to moderate (a quality or condition) in force or intensity; alleviate

negligible *adj.* 微不足道的

not significant or important enough to be worth considering; trifling

proliferate *vi.* 激增

to increase or spread at a rapid rate

Phrases

border enforcement	边境执法
compliance reviews and visits	合规审查和访问
cost-competitiveness	成本竞争力
cross border movement	跨境转移

Chapter 5 Free Ports and Foreign-Trade Zones

Customs and Border Protection	美国海关和边境保护局
exempt from	豁免,免除
high value-added	高附加值的
import quota	进口配额
initial cost	创办成本
labor-intensive	劳动密集型的
on a case-by-case basis	逐个地;视个案而定
subject to	缴纳(税款)

Key terms

A Free Trade Agreement (FTA)	自由贸易协议
ad valorem taxes	从价税
customs territory	关税区
economic liberty	经济自由
excise tax	消费税
internal revenue tax	内地税
multilateral tariff agreements	多边关税协议
tax holiday	免税期
tax rebates	出口退税
trademark rights	商标产权

Post-Reading Activities

I. Answer the following questions based on what you have read in the text.

1. In which situation goods in the free port should be charged with duties?
2. What is the difference between Free Trade Zone and Free-Trade Area?
3. Why has Free Trade Zones been criticized?
4. What can be placed in Free Trade Zones in the United States?
5. What are responsibilities of CBP?

II. Look at the terms in the left-hand column and find the correct definitions in the right-hand column. Copy the corresponding letters in the blanks.

1. _____ Free Trade Agreement (FTA)   A. it is sponsored by general-purpose zones, but typically involve a single firm's site which is used for more extensive manufacturing/processing or warehousing/distribution that cannot easily be accomplished in a general-purpose zone

2. _____ General-purpose zone   B. provided the means for U.S. firms to shift production of their products overseas, and for foreign-based firms to more easily compete in the U.S. market

3. _____ Subzone   C. a legally binding agreement between two or more countries to reduce or eliminate barriers to trade, and facilitate the cross border movement of goods and services between the territories of the Parties

4. _____ "twin plant" program   D. one of two key pieces of legislation passed in 1934 in an attempt to mitigate some of the destructive effects of the Smoot-Hawley Tariffs, which had been imposed in 1930. And it was created to "expedite and encourage foreign commerce" in the United States

5. _____ The Foreign-Trade Zones Act   E. it involves public facilities that can be used by more than one firm, and are most commonly ports or industrial parks used by small to medium sized businesses for warehousing/distribution and some processing/assembly

Chapter 5 Free Ports and Foreign-Trade Zones

III. Translate the following sentences into Chinese.

1. A free trade zone (FTZ) is a specified area within the territorial jurisdiction of a country where there is either a minimum or no customs control on entry or exit of goods. A free port (FP) is characterized by its whole harbor plants (sheet of water, quays, wharves, warehouses, factories, etc.) that are considered by law outside the customs boundaries. FTZ's and FP's are not subject to such standard government restrictions on trade such as Customs treatment, banking laws, taxation, labour laws and economical laws and transactions.

2. The main idea behind creation of Free Trade Zones is to facilitate cross-border trade by removing obstacles imposed by customs regulations. Free Trade Zones ensure faster turnaround of planes and ships by lowering custom related formalities.

3. FTZs prove to be beneficial both for the importers and exporters, as these zones are designed to reduce labor cost and tax related expenditures. Free Trade Zones help the traders to utilize the available business opportunities in the best possible way. FTZs promote export-oriented industries. These zones also help to increase foreign exchange earnings. Employment opportunities created by free trade zones help to reduce unemployment problem in the less developed economies.

4. The General Agreement on Tariffs and Trade (known by its acronym "GATT") became the working model by which more than 120 nations participated in round after round of multilateral tariff reductions for nearly 50 years. From 1946 until 1995, the GATT served to break down the barriers to trade on a worldwide basis. This expansion of trade played a critical part in the 50-year economic boom in member countries following the end of the Second World War.

5. FTZ activity must not conflict with U.S. trade policy or harm domestic industry or other domestic plants outside of zones. The FTZ Board requires that zone manufacturing activity result in a significant public benefit and a net positive economic effect. In addition, the U.S. Customs Service supervises all zone activity and ensures that all customs and FTZ Board requirements are observed.

IV. Translate the following sentences into English with the words given.

1. 对在自由贸易园区内生产活动的审批会视个案情况而定。(on a case-by-case basis)
2. 很多应缴纳内地税的产品不能在自由贸易园区内生产。(subject to)

3. 在自由贸易园区内商品无需缴纳美国关税或消费税。(duty or excise tax)
4. 自由贸易园区项目提供了减轻自由贸易成本的途径。(mitigate)
5. 因为向跨国公司提供了更多的经济自由,建立自由贸易区受到了批评。(economic liberty)

Chapter 6

International Trade Barrier

> **Pre-reading questions:**
> 1. Do you have an idea about Tariff barriers?
> 2. What on earth is Non-Tariff barriers?
> 3. What are the government's basic purposes in establishing tariffs and quotas on imported goods and instituting exchange controls?
> 4. In what way may a foreign country restrict imports?
> 5. How many types of import quotas are in use today? And what are they?

Text

Introduction

In recent years, the international trade has developed rapidly. But at the same time the products are suffering the barriers of international trade frequently, which greatly influence the export and import in the worldwide.

Trade barriers are government-induced restrictions on international trade.

Most trade barriers work on the same principle: the imposition of some sort of cost on trade that raises the price of the traded products. If two or more nations repeatedly use trade barriers against each other, then a trade war results.

Economists generally agree that trade barriers are detrimental and decrease overall economic efficiency, this can be explained by the theory of comparative advantage. In theory, free trade involves the removal of all such barriers, except perhaps those considered necessary for health or national security. In practice, however, even those countries promoting free trade heavily subsidize certain industries, such as agriculture and steel.

Trade barriers are often criticized for the effect they have on the developing world. Because rich-country players call most of the shots and set trade policies, goods such as crops that developing countries are best at producing still face high barriers. Trade barriers such as taxes on food imports or subsidies for farmers in developed economies lead to overproduction and dumping on world markets, thus lowering prices and hurting poor-country farmers. Tariffs also tend to be anti-poor, with low rates for raw commodities and high rates for labor-intensive processed goods. The Commitment to Development Index measures the effect that rich country trade policies actually have on the developing world.

Another negative aspect of trade barriers is that it would cause a limited choice of products and would therefore force customers to pay higher prices and accept inferior quality.

The trade barriers can take many forms, including Tariff barriers and Non-tariff barriers to trade.

Tariffs

A tariff is a tax levied by a government on goods imported into that country. The words tariff, duty, and customs are generally used interchangeably.

The tariff increases the price at which the goods are sold in the importing country and therefore makes them less competitive with locally produced goods. The tariff also provides the government with extra tax revenue. In addition to that, tariffs can effectively protect local industry by driving up the price of an imported item that competes with domestic products. This practice allows domestic producers either to charge higher prices for their goods or to capitalize on their own lighter taxes by charging lower prices and attracting more customers. Tariffs are often used to protect infant industries or to safeguard older industries that are in decline. They are sometimes criticized for imposing hidden costs on domestic consumers and encouraging inefficiency in domestic industries.

A tariff may be one of the four kinds: ad valorem, specific, alternative or compound. An ad valorem, the kind most commonly used, is one that is calculated as a percentage of the value of the imported good — for example, 10, 25 or 35 percent. They may be based, depending on the country, either on the value of the goods landed at the port of destination, or on the value of the goods at the port in the country of origin. A specific duty is a tax of so much local currency per unit of the goods imported based on weight, number, length, volume, or other unit of measurement. An alternative duty is where both an ad valorem duty and a specific one are prescribed for a product, with the requirement that the more onerous one shall apply. A compound duty is a comb-ination of an ad valorem duty and specific duty.

Ad. valorem duties are levied on most manufactured goods. This is because the monetary value of the duty varies in accordance with most manufactured goods — thus keeping duties up with inflation. Specific duties are often levied on foodstuffs and raw materials. Compound duties are imposed on manufactured goods which contain raw materials that are themselves subject to import duty. The specific part of the compound duty is levied as protection for the local raw material industry (for example, cotton growing) and the ad valorem part, as protection for the local manufacturing industry (for example, textiles).

Non-tariff Barriers to Trade

Contrary to tariff measures which are normally transparent, non-tariff barriers (NTBs) are often more difficult to detect because they are hidden in rules and practices that have a perfectly legitimate objective. Furthermore, NTBs can have more trade-restrictive effects than tariffs, which raise the cost of a given product, and go as far as excluding the goods from a market altogether.

Their use has risen sharply after the WTO rules led to a very significant reduction in tariff use. Some non-tariff trade barriers are expressly permitted in very limited circumstances, when they are deemed necessary to protect health, safety, or sanitation, or to protect depletable natural resources. In other forms, they are criticized as a means to evade free trade rules such as those of the World Trade Organization (WTO), the European Union (EU), or North American Free Trade Agreement (NAFTA) that restrict the use of tariffs.

Some of non-tariff barriers are not directly related to foreign economic regulations, but nevertheless they have a significant impact on foreign-economic activity and foreign trade between countries.

Trade between countries is referred to trade in goods, services and factors of production. Non-tariff barriers to trade include import quotas, special licenses, unreasonable standards for the quality of goods, export restrictions, limiting the activities of state trading, export subsidies, countervailing duties, technical barriers to trade, sanitary and phyto-sanitary measures, rules of origin, etc.

Licenses

The most common instruments of direct regulation of imports (and sometimes export) are licenses and quotas. Almost all industrialized countries apply these non-tariff methods. The license system requires that a state (through specially authorized office) issues permits for foreign trade transactions of import and export commodities included in the lists of licensed merchandises. The use of licensing systems as an instrument for foreign trade regulation is based on a number of international level standards agreements. In particular, these agreements include some provisions of the General Agreement on Tariffs and Trade and the Agreement on Import Licensing Procedures, concluded under the GATT.

Import Quotas

An exporter may find that the foreign country restricts import not only by means of tariffs but also by quantitative restrictions. These usually take the form of import quotas for each particular product. Once the quota for the period has been filled, no more import license are issued. There are three main types of import quotas in use today: unilateral quotas, negotiated bilateral or multilateral quotas, and tariff quotas.

Foreign Exchange Restrictions

Some countries restrict imports by limiting the amount of exchange, or foreign currency, available to pay for them. Often imports are classified into essential and non-essential imports while a more limited amount of foreign currency is made available at a much higher rate of exchange for the luxury items such as foreign cars and cosmetics. While complete exchange control, anyone wishing to obtain foreign exchange must secure permission from the government. Such a system permits the government to restrict the demand for scarce foreign exchange and to ration it out among different needs.

Bureaucratic Delays at Customs

Sometimes the exporter finds that their goods are held up at foreign ports because of inexplicable delays by customs officials. These are the result of a deliberate government policy to restrict imports. The customs may argue that the documentation or marking of the goods is not exactly as required. Should the Customs authorities decide to inspect thoroughly each item imported, rather than just a sample, there will be horrendous delays.

Import Deposits

Another example of foreign trade regulations is import deposits. Import deposits is a form of deposit, which the importer must pay the bank for a definite period of time (non-interest bearing deposit) in an amount equal to all or part of the cost of imported goods.

At the national level, administrative regulation of capital movements is carried out mainly within a framework of bilateral agreements, which include a clear definition of the legal regime, the procedure for the admission of investments and investors. It is determined by mode (fair and equitable, national, most-favored-nation), order of nationalization and compensation, transfer profits and capital repatriation and dispute resolution.

Some foreign countries refuse to buy goods from a country or firm that displeases it in one way or another. The most obvious current example is the Arab boycott of firms trading with Israel. Technical barriers are phony standards set for imported goods designed to exclude them from the domestic market. As another example, unnecessary health regulations may be used to exclude foreign good products.

Vocabulary

barrier *n.* 壁垒
any condition that makes it difficult to make progress or to achieve an objective

detrimental *adj.* 有害的；不利的
causing harm or injury

subsidy *n.* 补贴
a grant paid by a government to an enterprise

overproduction *n.* 生产过剩
too much production or more than expected

dumping *n.* 倾销
selling goods abroad at a price below that charged in the domestic market

inferior *adj.* 较次的,低劣的

one of lesser rank or station or quality
levy *v.* 征收
to impose and collect
interchangeably *adv.* 可互换地
in an interchangeable manner
revenue *n.* 收入，税收
government income due to taxation
capitalize *v.* 利用；积累资本
to take advantage of
safeguard *v.* 保护
to protect
ad valorem *adj.* 从价的，按照价值的
in proportion to the estimated value of the goods taxed
specific *adj.* 从量的
in proportion to the estimated weight, number, length, volume of the goods taxed
inflation *n.* 通货膨胀
a general and progressive increase in prices
alternative *adj.* 二选一的
one of a number of things from which only one can be chosen
compound *adj.* 复合的
consisting of two or more substances or ingredients or elements or parts
land *v.* 带上岸或卸上岸
to arrive on shore
volume *n.* 体积
the amount of 3-dimensional space occupied by an object
measurement *n.* 度量衡制度
the act or process of measuring
onerous *adj.* 有麻烦的或有压力的，难以负担的
not easily borne; wearing
apply *v.* 适用

to be pertinent or relevant or applicable

monetary *adj.* 货币的

relating to or involving money

foodstuff *n.* 食品

a substance that can be used or prepared for use as food

impose *v.* 征收

to levy

compensatory *adj.* 补偿性的

compensating for

discourage *v.* 阻止

to prevent

transparent *adj.* 透明的

able to be seen through with clarity

detect *v.* 察觉

to discover or determine the existence, presence, or fact of

legitimate *adj.* 合法的

recognized as lawful

sanitation *n.* 卫生检疫

the state of being clean and conducive to health

depletable *adj.* 可消耗的

capable of being depleted

evade *v.* 规避,逃避

to avoid or try to avoid fulfilling, answering, or performing (duties, questions, or issues)

sanitary *adj.* 卫生的

be healthful

inexplicable *adj.* 不明原因的,无法说明的

incapable of being explained or accounted for

deliberate *adj.* 蓄意的;深思熟虑的;慎重的

carefully thought out in advance

authorities *n.* 当局,权力

the organization that is the governing authority of a political unit

inspect *v.* 检查,检验

to look over carefully

horrendous *adj.* 可怕的,令人吃惊的

causing fear or dread or terror

deposit *n.* 押金

money deposited in a bank

bilateral *adj.* 双边的

having two sides or parts

repatriation *n.* 把(海外利润)调回国内

the act of returning to the country of origin

boycott *n.* 抵制,联合拒绝购买

a group's refusal to have commercial dealings with some organization in protest against its policies

phony *adj.* 不诚实或欺骗的

fraudulent; having a misleading appearance

Phrase

in theory	从理论上来说
in particular	尤其,特别
by means of	通过
carry out	执行,进行
rather than	而不是

Key terms

trade barriers	贸易壁垒
comparative advantage	比较优势
tariffs/duties/customs	关税

Chapter 6 International Trade Barrier

tariffs barriers	关税壁垒
non-tariff barriers	非关税壁垒
raw commodities	原材料商品
labor-intensive processed goods	劳动密集型商品
trade policies	贸易政策
tax revenue	税收收入
local industry	本土产业
domestic products	本国产品
ad valorem duties	从价税
specific duties	从量税
alternative duties	选择税
compound duties	复合税
manufactured goods	产成品
raw materials	原材料
manufacturing industry	制造业
natural resources	自然资源
import quotas	进口配额
special licenses	特种许可证
standards for the quality of goods	商品质量标准
export restrictions	出口限制
export subsidies	出口补贴
countervailing duty	反补贴关税
unilateral quotas	单边配额
negotiated bilateral or multilateral quotas	双边配额
tariff quotas	关税配额
foreign currency	外币
Bureaucratic delays at customs	繁杂的海关手续
technical barriers	技术壁垒
sanitary and phyto-sanitary measures	动植物卫生检疫
rules of origin	原产地规定

licensing systems	许可证制
foreign trade regulation	外贸管制
Foreign exchange restrictions	外汇管制
import deposits	进口押金制
bilateral agreements	双边协议
most-favored-nation	最惠国
boycott	联合抵制
country of origin	原产国

Post-Reading Activities

I. Answer the following questions based on what you have read in the text.

1. What are the government's basic purposes in establishing tariffs and quotas on imported goods and instituting exchange controls?.

2. On what kind of goods are Ad valorem levied? Why?

3. On what kind of goods are specific duties levied?

4. In what way may a foreign country restrict imports?

5. Once the quota for the period has been filled, what will happen?

II. Look at the terms in the left-hand column and find the correct definitions in the right-hand column. Copy the corresponding letters in the blanks.

1. _____ non-tariff barriers   A. a tax levied by a government on goods imported into that country

2. _____ tariffs   B. the duty is calculated as a percentage of the value of the imported goods

3. _____ Ad valorem duties   C. a tax for the goods imported based on weight, number, length, volume, or other unit of measurement

4. _____ compound duties   D. a duty that combines an ad valorem duty and

5. _____ specific duties
6. _____ foreign exchange restrictions
7. _____ import deposit

specific duty

E. restricting imports by limiting the amount of exchange, or foreign currency, available to pay for them

F. a form of deposit, which the importer must pay the bank for a definite period of time (non-interest bearing deposit) in an amount equal to all or part of the cost of imported goods

G. one kind of barriers that are often more difficult to detect because they are hidden in rules and practices and that can have more trade-restrictive effects than tariffs

III. Translate the following sentences into Chinese.

1. But at the same time the products are suffering the barriers of international trade frequently, which greatly influence the export and import in the worldwide.

2. Economists generally agree that trade barriers are detrimental and decrease overall economic efficiency, this can be explained by the theory of comparative advantage.

3. Trade barriers such as taxes on food imports or subsidies for farmers in developed economies lead to overproduction and dumping on world markets, thus lowering prices and hurting poor-country farmers.

4. Another negative aspect of trade barriers is that it would cause a limited choice of products and would therefore force customers to pay higher prices and accept inferior quality.

5. A tariff is a tax levied by a government on goods imported into that country. The words tariff, duty, and customs are generally used interchangeably.

6. A tariff may be one of the four kinds: ad valorem, specific, alternative or compound.

7. Contrary to tariff measures which are normally transparent, non-tariff barriers (NTBs) are often more difficult to detect because they are hidden in rules and practices that have a perfectly legitimate objective.

8. An exporter may find that the foreign country restricts import not only by means of tariffs but also by quantitative restrictions. These usually take the form of import quotas for each particular

product.

9. Once the quota for the period has been filled, no more import license are issued. There are three main types of import quotas in use today: unilateral quotas, negotiated bilateral or multilateral quotas, and tariff quotas.

10. At the national level, administrative regulation of capital movements is carried out mainly within a framework of bilateral agreements, which include a clear definition of the legal regime, the procedure for the admission of investments and investors.

IV. Translate the following sentences into English with the words given.

1. 关税是对进口和出口商品征收的一种税收,有时称为海关税。(levy/impose)

2. 收入性关税(revenue tariff)提供一些有限的保护,而保护性关税(protective tariff)带来一些少量的收入。

3. 我们不排除(exclude)一些好战者(warmonger)将会冒险(run the risk of)发动一场新的战争的可能性。

4. 外贸管制的一个例子就是进口押金制。(import deposits.)

5. 经济学家认为贸易壁垒是有害的,它会损害整体经济效益(detrimental)

Chapter 7

The Sino-U. S. Trade Relation

> **Pre-reading questions:**
> 1. What's wrong with the Sino-U. S. Trade Relation?
> 2. How many problems do you think are there between China and the U. S. ?
> 3. What's a threat to the U. S. Homeland Security?
> 4. What's wrong with the U. S. Statistics?
> 5. What's the prospect of the Sino-U. S. Trade Relation?

Text

Introduction

Forty years ago, the Shanghai Communique was published here. It is a milestone in the history of China-U. S. relations and opened a new chapter of exchanges and cooperation between China and United States. Today, standing on the new historical start-point, China and U. S. are working together to build a cooperative partnership based on mutual respect and mutual benefit along the direction mapped out by leaders of both countries.

Meanwhile, at this moment of "no perplexities", China-U. S. relationship is still facing some perplexities. For example, the United States of America often initiates countervailing, anti-dumping investigation to China; and also makes use of green trade barriers, intellectual property issues, technical barriers to trade and other restrictions to restrict imports of Chinese products. It keeps urging on us to take more efforts to promote the lasting development of this relationship along a healthy and stable course.

Recently, the American Secretary of Commerce, Don Evans, has indicated that he is willing to negotiate with China on how to solve problems in the bilateral trade relation.

Since the beginning of this year, the U.S. has brought out seven anti-dumping cases against China, involving a huge value worth $1.6 billion. These cases have severely disrupted the normal trade order between China and the United States. What's wrong with the bilateral economic and trade relation that has been the foundation of the overall Sino-U.S. relationship? Let us take the example of the price of a pair of leather boots to investigate the causes for these trade disputes.

The First Cause: Worries Over American Jobs Taken Away by Chinese Goods

We here have a pair of exquisitely made leather boots for females. Its price at the time of export is $20. It is made by a shoe factory in China's Zhejiang Province. Not long ago, at the trade show in New York organized for Chinese products, an American import/export merchant liked the boots and decided to offer an order. Next year, when this pair of boots appears in a store in New York, the price will be $100. According to another import/export merchant, the big difference between $20 and $100 will be shared by the import/export merchant, the wholesaler and the retailer. If the pair of boots attracts attention of a famous shoe brand in the U.S., then slight changes in design and craftsmanship can be made. It will sell for up to $200. This simple fact shows that overwhelming portion of the profits from goods "Made in China" are taken by the American side.

Cheap and good products made in China have reduced America's pressure from inflation, which further benefits the consumers, enriches the import/export merchants, wholesale and retail business circles. Then, why is it that there always are some people who frequently try to stop the import of Chinese products? Due to structural changes within manufacturing industry in the United States, unemployment has increased in some factories that are fast becoming parts of the "sunset" industries, with a drop in overall competitiveness. As a result, a scapegoat must be found somewhere and China thus has become a convenient target. It is believed that China has taken away their jobs. They have requested that the American government put restrictions on imports from China so that they can protect themselves.

The Second Cause: Fear of China's Advance in Hi-Tech as a Threat to the U.S. Homeland Security

Because of the different political system and ideology, some Americans always tend to view

China's economic development through tinted glasses. The San Jose Mercury News commentator Snyder points out in an article entitled "Transfer of Technology to China Threatens U. S. National Security," that although China no longer is an enemy of the U. S., it still is a strategic competitor that does not share America's system of values; that the U. S. does not know which direction China is going, nor does it know eventually in what areas China and the U. S. will have clash of interests; that therefore when China is leaping upward to higher layers of advanced technologies, the Americans are justified to be concerned, especially when it comes to the area of military applications.

For a long period, the so-called monitoring and control measures of the United States have become a big obstacle in the Sino-U. S. bilateral trade. Some Americans believe that even if the restrictions on Hi-Tech transfer to China are lifted, the trade deficit with China would still not go away. Charlene Barshefsky, the former U. S. Trade Representative, states that the U. S. has done some calculations on this matter and reached the conclusion that lifting the restrictions would increase only 3% of U. S. export to China. But in reality, these analyses are still pigeonholed by some dogmas.

Trade should be a bilateral exchange that is based on long-term stability. It cannot be measured by one lump sum purchase of goods, which is especially true in the Hi-Tech industry. Trade also includes other aspects such as services, training, exports and R&D of auxiliary products. But the regulations by the United States government are remarkably vague, making the process of implementing them very complicated. Some factories have complained that businesses are forced to invite experts to guess and analyze whether their products for export to China, especially those dual-use products that can be converted for military applications, are compliant with the U. S. regulations. Earlier this year, the U. S. State Department charged the Boeing Company and the Hughes Inc. with leaking satellite technologies to China, and demanded that the two companies pay fines as high as $60 million. In reality, the charge of leaking technologies to China can never be substantiated. The problem is that the two companies violated the U. S. government's so-called "operational procedures." Many businesses have even given up on some products altogether that would have been eligible for export to China.

The Third Cause: Serious Flaws in the U. S. Statistics

According to the U. S. statistics, there is a huge trade deficit against the American side. But by Chinese statistics, this is not the case. The Chinese numbers point to the fact that between January and September of this year, China has a trade surplus with the United States of $40 billion, with increases in exports by 31.4% and in imports by 26.1%. Yet the American statistics indicates that between January and August of this year, the United States has a trade deficit with China worth $77 billion. Why is there such a huge discrepancy between these numbers? This is because China's numbers do not include the products that went to the U.S. market through Hong Kong and Macau, while the U.S. statistics adopts a method of counting goods by their origin of manufacturing, i.e., which country should be counted as the place from which the import comes depends solely on where the products are manufactured or substantially re-made.

Since the 1990s, one important reason why China's exports have increased has been the increase in its manufacturing trade. Yet the American side has insisted on using its own extremely unjustified method of statistics, which includes entre pot trade as "origin of manufacturing" trade. The reason this is unjustified is because, of the price at the time of export, the portion of profit that goes to the original manufacturers constitutes only a small portion. For example, the price of $20 at the time of export transaction for the same pair of leather boots we mentioned at the beginning, if exported to the United States via Hong Kong, should not be counted all as China's. If it is, as being currently practiced by the U.S., China's export value will be tremendously exaggerated.

In recent years, the multinationals in the U.S. have been expanding rapidly to the rest of the world, with many medium-and small-sized businesses following suit. Here we only have statistics from five years ago, but they are revealing. In 1998, American businesses had 8 million employees worldwide outside of the U.S. This is more than the total number of employment for the entire manufacturing industries in the overwhelming majority of the nations in the world. Only 30% of the products by America's overseas business branches were sold in the U.S., the rest were sold mostly in other developed countries.

With an increasing number of American businesses going to China, China is becoming the general assembly base for these American companies' products. In 1994, the China branches of all American businesses shipped back to the U.S. products worth $5.1 billion. In 2001, the same number reached $18.5 billion. The fact that some American businesses shift their production lines to China has created enormous pressure to their domestic competitors, causing, to certain extent, fierce competition among American businesses, and forcing these businesses to speed up the process of moving their production lines overseas. Thus, a significant portion of the profits generated from the products made in China but sold in the U. S. have been taken by American businesses. Again, take the same pair of leather boots as an example. When it is packaged with an American brand name, naturally it is the American company that makes most of the profit out of it. In fact, more than half of China's popular export, the textiles, have entered the U. S. market in this fashion.

The Forth Cause: Refusing to Recognize the Benefits that American Businesses Have Received

As early as 20 years ago, the United States entered the post-industrial age, with Hi-Tech and the service industry becoming the economic locomotives. This change in America's economic structure is an important reason why there has been increase in Chinese products in the U. S. market. The general public feels they are attacked by a deluge of Chinese made products everywhere. But the added value of Chinese goods is small, constituting only a small portion of the entire U. S. economy. According to the U. S. statistics, in 2002, the U. S. bought from China products worth $125 billion; the total volume of the U. S. economy was $10.4 trillion. That is to say, for very dollar the Americans spent that year, only a little more than a penny was spent on Chinese goods.

Facing increasing Chinese products, the American consumers have a dilemma. When they can buy cheap and good Chinese products in the supermarkets, they of course are happy. But if the consumer himself is an employee of the industry that manufactures the same product, or if he is already laid off, he may unleash his discontent onto the Chinese products. The key point here is that after China, as the largest developing country in the world, entered the World Trade Organization, its not just China that needs to learn new things to catch up, developed countries such as the United States should too. The latest trade-related incidents have shown that the Americans have much homework to do in order to catch up. For example, they should know that the increase in America's unemployment is not a result of the increase in Chinese imports. According to the U. S. statistics, despite the recent setbacks suffered by the American economy, the output of the American manufacturing industry has increased by 40% in the past ten years, doubling what it produced in the 1970s. This is because the American factories are hiring fewer and fewer workers, worker's skills are constantly enhancing and one worker can finish what might take several workers to accomplish in the past. Unemployment is an American dilemma, as well as a dilemma for China. Chinese businesses are facing a far more severe competition as a result of American entrance into China's labor market.

They have to endure a far heavier burden of unemployment than their American counterparts.

The Prospect he Sino-U. S. Trade Relation: Volume of Sino-U. S. Bilateral Trade Will Only Increase But not Decrease

By American statistics, the value of bilateral trade between the two countries was $95.9 million in 1972. Last year, it reached $120 billion. The rate of increase is incredibly rapid in terms of the total value of trade. In spite of this, however, there still exists great potential for further developments in the Sino-U. S. economic and trade relation. In the long run, the volume of Sino-U. S. bilateral trade will only increase, but not decrease. Due to the differences in their political and economic systems, it is expected that trade disputes will continue to exist. A former president of the National Committee on U. S. -China Trade Relations said recently that over the past thirty years there have been constant changes in U. S. -China relation, and in the next thirty years this situation may not cease to exist. China's role in world economy is rising steadily. The style and contents of the U. S. -China relation are changing as well. Both sides view and expect each other as a world power, with an increasingly sophisticated system of mutual observations. In overcoming a variety of profound problems faced by mankind, and in encountering separate set of challenges to their respective economic and political systems, both countries have a long way to go.

Vocabulary

milestone *n.* 里程碑
stone put at the side of a road showing distances in miles
perplexity *n.* 困惑, 混乱
state of being perplexed; bewilderment
commerce *n.* 商业, 贸易, 交易
the buying and selling of goods
indicate *v.* 指示, 表明, 象征
to show something in a way that may not be quite clear
negotiate *v.* 谈判, 协商
to try to come to an agreement through talking

bilateral *adj.* 双方的,双边的
including or concerning two people or two countries
anti-dumping *adj.* 反营销政策的
disrupt *v.* 中断,扰乱
to stop something from continuing as expected
overall *adj.* 全部的,总的
including everything or the whole of something
leather *n.* 皮革
treated animal skin used for making things like shoes and bags
boot *n.* 长筒靴
a shoe that covers your whole foot and ankle
dispute *n.* 争论,辩论,纠纷
an argument or quarrel, especially an official one
exquisitely *adv.* 优美的,精致的
extremely beautiful, delicate, or sensitive
import *n.* 进口
to bring goods in from another country
export *n.* 出口
to send things to another country, usually to sell them
merchant *n.* 商人,外贸批发商
a person who buys and sells goods, usually in large amounts, especially from and to foreign countries
wholesaler *n.* 批发商
a businessman who sells goods wholesale
retailer *n.* 零售商
a person who sells goods to the public
brand *n.* 商标,牌子
a class of goods which is the product of a particular firm or producer
craftsmanship *n.* 技术,技艺
skilled workmanship

overwhelming *adj.* 巨大的,压倒一片的
very large or very great
portion *n.* 部分,一份
an amount or share of something
profit *n.* 利润,赢利,收益
money which is earned by doing business, after all the costs are taken from it
inflation *n.* 通货膨胀
general rise in prices
enrich *v.* 使(某人)富裕
to make someone rich
frequently *adv.* 经常,时常
often
structural *adj.* 结构上的
of or concerning structure
manufacture *v.* 用机器大量制造(货物)
make (goods) on a large scale using machinery
unemployment *n.* 失业人数
the number of people in a society without a job
competitiveness *n.* 竞争力
scapegoat *n.* 替罪羊,代人受过的人
a person who is blamed for something that others have done or have also done
convenient *adj.* 便利的,合宜的
suited to your needs or to the situation
target *n.* 目标,靶子
an object, building, or place which is aimed at, especially with a gun or bomb
restriction *n.* 限制,约束
restricting or being restricted
homeland *n.* 祖国,故乡
the country where you were born
security *n.* 安全,安全感

the state of being secure

ideology *n.* 思想体系

a set of ideas typical of a social or political group

tint *n.* 浅色,淡色

a pale or delicate shade of a colour

commentator *n.* 解说员,评论员

person who comments

entitle *v.* 给(书、剧本、电影或画)题名

to give someone the right to have or do something

transfer *v.* 转移,迁移

to move from one place or job to another within the same organization

threaten *v.* 危及,威胁到(某事物)

seem likely to harm, spoil, or ruin something

strategic *adj.* 战略性的

the science of studying numbers in order to get facts or information

surplus *n.* 盈余,剩余

an amount that is more than what is needed or used

discrepancy *n.* 差异,不符合,不一致

difference between things that should be the same

solely *adv.* 仅仅,独一无二

only

substantially *adv.* 大量地,可观地

by a large amount

transaction *n.* 交易,要处理之事

a piece of business

tremendously *adv.* 极大地

very great in size, amount, or degree

exaggerate *v.* 夸大,夸张

to make something seem larger or more important than it really is

multinational *adj.* 跨国公司的,多国的

involving many countries

assembly *adv.* 集会，集合
the meeting of a group of people for a particular purpose

domestic *adj.* 本国的，国内的
relating to your own country or some particular country

textile *n.* 纺织品
any material made by weaving

locomotive *n.* 火车头，机车
a railway engine

deluge *n.* 大量同时发生的事物
a very large number of things which happen at the same time

volume *n.* （某物）的量
the amount of something

trillion *num.* 万亿

dilemma *n.* 困境，进退两难的窘境
a difficult situation in which you have to choose between two possible actions

unleash *v.* 发出，发泄
to allow strong or violent forces or feelings to come out

discontent *adj.* 不满，不满足
the feeling of not being happy or satisfied

setback *n.* 退步，倒退
a return to a less good position

accomplish *v.* 做成功，完成（某事）
to succeed in doing something

sophisticated *adj.* 复杂的，精密的
not simple

mutual *adj.* 相互的，共同的
shared by two people and directed towards each other

Phrases

be willing to	愿意做某事
at the time of	在……时候
due to	因为,由于
no longer	不再
reach the conclusion	得出结论
to certain extent	达到某种程度
speed up	(使)加速
lay off	解雇(某人)
as well as	另外,而且
as a result of	作为……的结果,所以
in the long run	终究,最终,从长远来看
a variety of	种种,各种

Key terms

countervailing	反补贴
anti-dumping investigation	反倾销调查
green trade barriers	绿色贸易壁垒
intellectual property issues	知识产权问题
technical barriers to trade	技术贸易壁垒
secretary of commerce	商务秘书
anti-dumping cases	反倾销案例
bilateral economic and trade relation	双边经贸关系
bilateral trade relation	双边贸易关系
inflation	通货膨胀
import merchant	进口商

export merchant	出口商
the wholesaler	批发商
the retailer	零售商
transfer of technology	技术转让
strategic competitor	战略竞争者
hi-tech	高科技
trade deficit	财政赤字；贸易逆差
the U.S. homeland security	美国国土安全
medium-and small-sized businesses	中小企业
post-industrial age	后工业时代
world trade organization	世界贸易组织
labor market	劳动力市场
national committee	国家委员会

Post-Reading Activities

I. Answer the following questions based on what you have read in the text.

1. How many problems are there between China and the U.S.?
2. What has become a big obstacle in the Sino-U.S. bilateral trade? Why?
3. How do the American consumers react to the increasing Chinese products?
4. What's the prospect?

II. Look at the terms in the left-hand column and find the correct definitions in the right-hand column. Copy the corresponding letters in the blanks.

1. _____ anti-dumping   A. it mainly engages in research & development, design of three categories of products

2. _____ inflation   B. defend the action of offering large amounts of stock with little or no concern for price or market effect

3. _____ R&D of auxiliary products   C. a difference between conflicting facts or claims or opinions
4. _____ dual-use   D. release his dissatisfaction to
5. _____ discrepancy   E. the overall or specific increase in the cost of a good or service
6. _____ unleash his discontent onto   F. the problems that need much study or thought
7. _____ profound problems   G. a term often used in politics and diplomacy to refer to technology which can be used for both peaceful and military aims

III. Translate the following sentences into English.

1. Cheap and good products made in China have reduced America's pressure from inflation, which further benefits the consumers, enriches the import/export merchants, wholesale and retail business circles.

2. Why is it that there always are some people who frequently try to stop the import of Chinese products? Due to structural changes within manufacturing industry in the United States, unemployment has increased in some factories that are fast becoming parts of the "sunset" industries, with a drop in overall competitiveness.

3. For a long period, the so-called monitoring and control measures of the United States have become a big obstacle in the Sino-U.S. bilateral trade. Some Americans believe that even if the restrictions on Hi-Tech transfer to China are lifted, the trade deficit with China would still not go away.

4. Some factories have complained that businesses are forced to invite experts to guess and analyze whether their products for export to China, especially those dual-use products that can be converted for military applications, are compliant with the U.S. regulations.

5. According the U.S. statistics, there is a huge trade deficit against the American side. But by Chinese statistics, this is not the case. The Chinese numbers point to the fact that between January and September of this year, China has a trade surplus with the United States of $40 billion, with increases in exports by 31.4% and in imports by 26.1%.

IV. Translate the following sentences into English with the words given.

1. 美国和中国愿意就如何解决双边贸易问题进行谈判。(be willing to do sth.)

2. 由于不同的政治体系和意识形态，有些美国人总是倾向于用有色眼镜看待中国的经济发展。(due to)

3. 随着进入中国的美国商业数量的增加，中国逐渐成为美国公司产品的主要生产基地。(assembly base)

4. 由于美国人进入到了中国劳动力市场，中国商业正在面临着更严峻的竞争。(competition)

5. 中国在世界经济中的作用在稳步提升。(rise steadily)

Chapter 8

Terms of Payment

Pre-reading questions:
1. How do you keep your payment security in an international deal?
2. How much do you know about payment terms?
3. Do you know the meaning of open Account?
4. What is Documentary collection?
5. Why is L/C security for goods and services imported and exported?

Text

Introduction

Foreign companies can obtain bank references on prospective customers before undertaking business in a country, and to consider whether checks by commercial credit agencies are appropriate. Before agreeing to a method of payment it is best to contact the International Division of your bank. Although there will be companies who manage to secure payment in 60 days or less the period of credit offered by a supplier to a customer tends to be amongst the highest in Europe, anything from 90 to 120 days. The method of payment will need to be agreed upon when negotiating the contract. It will depend on the degree of commercial trust that exists between the parties involved and whether credit is offered or required by either party.

Terms of payment are one of the main trading conditions as well as an indispensable part in the international sales of goods. International payment terms are much more complicated and difficult compared with domestic transaction payment.

The unit aims at introducing payment instruments and the methods of payment of international trade. On finishing this unit, the reader will have an understanding of Terms of Payment.

Open Account

Most of the foreign trade is conducted on an Open Account basis—as the most simple, straight forward and flexible method available. However you must ensure that your customer is highly reputable, if business is to be conducted on this basis with, for example your invoice being sent direct to them along with documents and requesting payment within the stipulated term. If he pays by cheque all costs associated with clearing the payment are borne by the exporter. If your bank has an operating subsidiary in a country it may simplify payment by asking them to open a foreign currency account in the country.

Payments for open account can be made in three main ways:
Electronic funds transfer (i.e. SWIFT/IMT);
Bankers draft;
Buyer's own cheque.

Documentary Collection (or Cash against Documents)

Normally carried out through a bank and a slightly more secure method of trading than Open Account. The exporter delivers all the necessary documents to his own bank which then sends them to a bank in the importer's country. Documents are only released in accordance with the exporter's instructions, e.g. against sight payment, or acceptance of a term Bill of Exchange.

Unless the goods are consigned to a third party, the exporter risks loss until settlement is made, if the importer fails to take up documents by paying or accepting the Bill of Exchange, there is also an additional risk of a buyer subsequently dishonoring an accepted Bill of Maturity. As with Open Account the exporter may be able to insure against this by Credit Insurance.

Letter of Credit

1. Introduction of L/C

The Letter of Credit is the most effective means of ensuring payment. It is a useful way for companies to trade with each other until they build up a relationship of mutual trust.

A standard, commercial letter of credit (L/C) is a document issued mostly by a financial institution, used primarily in trade finance, which usually provides an irrevocable payment undertaking.

The L/C can also be source of payment for a transaction, meaning that redeeming the letter of credit will pay an exporter. Letters of credit are used primarily in international trade transactions of significant value, for deals between a supplier in one country and customer in another. They are also used in the land development process to ensure that approved public facilities (streets, sidewalks, storm water ponds, etc.) will be built.

The parties to a letter of credit are usually a beneficiary, who is to receive the money, the issuing bank, of whom the applicant is a client, and the advising bank of whom the beneficiary is a client. Almost all letters of credit are irrevocable, i. e., cannot be amended or cancelled without prior agreement of the beneficiary, the issuing bank and the confirming bank, if any. In executing a transaction, letters of credit incorporate functions common to giros and Traveler's cheques.

Typically, the documents a beneficiary has to present in order to receive payment include a commercial invoice, bill of lading, and documents proving the shipment was insured against loss or damage in transit. However, the list and form of documents is open to imagination and negotiation and might contain requirements to present documents issued by a neutral third party evidencing the quality of the goods shipped, or their place of origin.

The English name "letter of credit" derives from the French word "accreditation", a power to do something, which in turn is derivative of the Latin word "accreditivus", meaning trust. The Applicator opens L/C in accordance with the underlying contract of sale and the seller performs their duties to an extent that meets the requirements contained in the L/C.

Being an irrevocable undertaking of the issuing bank, L/C guarantees the proceeds. For the Beneficiary of the Credit provided, stipulated documents strictly complying with the provisions of the L/C, UCP 600 and other international standard banking practices, are presented to the issuing bank, then:

(1) If the Credit provides for sight payment—by payment at sight against compliant presentation.

(2) If the Credit provides for deferred payment—by payment on the maturity Date (s) determinable in accordance with the stipulations of the Credit; and of course undertaking to pay on due date and confirming maturity date at the time of compliant presentation.

(3) If the Credit provides for acceptance by the Issuing Bank—by acceptance of Draft (s) drawn by the Beneficiary on the Issuing Bank and payment at maturity of such tenor draft.

(4) If the Credit provides for acceptance by another drawee bank—by acceptance and payment at maturity Draft (s) drawn by the Beneficiary on the Issuing Bank in the event the drawee bank stipulated in the Credit does not accept Draft (s) drawn on it, or by payment of Draft (s) accepted but not paid by such drawee bank at maturity.

(5) If the Credit provides for negotiation by another bank—by payment without recourse to drawers and/or bona fide holders, Draft (s) drawn by the Beneficiary and/or document (s) presented under the Credit, (and so negotiated by the nominated bank).

Negotiation means the giving of value for Draft (s) and/or document (s) by the bank authorized to negotiate, via the nominated bank. Mere examination of the documents and forwarding the same to L/C issuing bank for reimbursement, without giving of value / agreed to give, does not constitute a negotiation.

2. Process of letter of credit

Letter of Credit is a payment mechanism, particularly used in international trade. The seller gets paid, not after the buyer has inspected the goods and approved them, but when the seller presents certain documents (typically a bill of lading evidencing shipment of the goods, an insurance policy for the goods, commercial invoice, etc.) to his bank. The bank has to verify that the documents presented are true, and whether they " on their face" appear to be consistent with each other and comply with the terms of the credit. After examination, the bank will pay the seller (or in L/C terms the beneficiary of the letter of credit).

Letter of Credit, Standard Example:

(1) Buyer and seller sign a purchase contract that stipulates payment by Letter of Credit. It is good practice to agree in the purchase contract which documents the seller/beneficiary has to present.

(2) The buyer/applicant goes to his bank (so called issuing bank) opening the credit to the benefit of the seller, in particular the buyer tells his bank which documents the beneficiary has to present, where and how, and the amount of the credit and details of payment (by sight, deferred sight payment, against acceptance or negotiation of drafts).

(3) The Issuing Bank, which is normally located in a foreign country, advises the beneficiary through a correspondence bank located in the country of the Beneficiary of the credit. So in step 3, the Issuing Bank issues the L/C and forwards it to the Advising Bank.

(4) The Advising Bank checks the apparent authenticity of the L/C and advises the L/C to the beneficiary.

(5) The Seller/Beneficiary checks if the L/C complies with the commercial agreements and if all terms and conditions specified in the L/C can be satisfied, then the seller ships the goods.

(6) The Beneficiary prepares the documents specified in the L/C, checks the documents for discrepancies in the L/C, draws the draft and presents the draft and the documents to the Advising Bank and presents the necessary documents to his local bank which pay him after examining them.

(7) The Advising Bank bears the draft and the documents against terms and conditions of the L/C and forwards them to the Issuing Bank.

(8) The Issuing Bank checks if the documents comply with the L/C and makes a payment (if the L/C is available by sight) on a certain date (if L/C is available by deferred payment).

3. Confirmed letter of credit

Confirmed Letter of Credit has the advantage that the payment obligation of the confirming bank is independent of the issuing bank. Buyers may obtain injunctions against the issuing bank in their home country to prevent the bank from honoring the L/C. Obtaining an injunction in a foreign country is more difficult.

4. Standby letter of credit?

A standby letter of credit is basically a bank guarantee. Previously, U. S. banks were not allowed to issue guarantees and circumvented this limitation by issuing a standby letter of credit where the beneficiary basically had to present negotiated documents to get paid. Most letters of credit, particularly in international transactions, are subject to the Uniform Customs and Practices for Documentary Credits (UCP) issued and published by the International Chamber of Commerce (ICC). The current revision, UCP 600, is publication No. 600 of the ICC and takes effect as of July 1, 2007. Since the ICC lacks legislative authority, meaning it is not the arm of, or authorized by any government, but rather a trade association, the UCP are not laws and have to be explicitly incorporated into individual transactions. Some countries and states have enacted statutes regarding Letters of Credit (see Article 5 U. S. Uniform Commercial Code). In international trade however, most parties choose to use the UCP.

5. Letters of credit discrepancies

In some cases, if the documents presented by the seller do not comply exactly with the requirements of the Letter of Credit, the buyer may agree to waive any discrepancies in the documents presented by the seller, and, if the bank agrees, a payment under the Letter of Credit can still occur. Credit professionals should be aware that all parties must agree to waive documentation discrepancies in order for the seller to be paid under the letter of credit.

What does this mean? It means that it is not enough for the buyer to waive the discrepancy or discrepancies. The issuing bank as well as the confirming bank (assuming the L/C is confirmed) must also agree to waive the discrepancies. This can present a problem if:

(1) The issuing bank is concerned about the creditworthiness of the applicant/buyer.

(2) If the confirming bank is concerned about the wisdom of its decision to confirm the Letter of Credit.

In either of these scenarios, a discrepancy in the documentation provided can be the reason/excuse/justification needed not to honor and fund the letter of credit. There is nothing unlawful about this scenario. Creditors need to know that once a discrepancy is found, if it cannot be corrected or if the discrepancy cannot be corrected within the time limitations attached to the Letter of Credit then all bets are off and the Letter of Credit offers no protection to the Seller.

Common Letter of Credit Discrepancies:

● The name and/or address of exporter or customer are misspelled.

● The Letter of Credit (L/C) expired prior to presentation of draft and other documents.

● The Bill of Lading evidences delivery prior to or after the date range stated in the L/C. For example, the bill of lading shipping date is later than that allowed in the L/C.

● Changes are included on the invoice that are not authorized in the L/C. For example, instructions in the L/C that are different from those on the invoice.

● The description of the goods is inconsistent, or there is an incomplete or inaccurate description of merchandise, price, and terms of payment.

● There are errors in the insurance documents.

● The invoice amount is not equal to the draft amount.

● Ports of loading and destination are not as specified in the L/C.

● The description of merchandise is not as stated in L/C. Omission of the word "about" or "approximately" (which allows for 10% variance) preceding the amount of credit.

● A document required by the L/C is not included in the package of documents presented by the seller to the confirming, advising or issuing bank.

● Documents are inconsistent as to general information such as volume, quality, etc.

● The invoice is not signed as required in the L/C, or marks and number on the invoice are different from those on other documents.

● Invoice value or draft exceeds amount available under Letter of Credit.

● Charges included in invoice are not authorized in Letter of Credit.

● Amount of insurance coverage is inadequate or coverage does not include risks required by the Letter of Credit.

● Insurance document is not endorsed and/or countersigned.

● Date of insurance policy or certificate is later than the date on bills of lading.

● Bills of lading are not clean—that is, they bear notations that qualify goods order and condition of merchandise or its packing.

- Bills of lading are not marked "on board" when so required by Letter of Credit.
- "On board" endorse mentor changes on bills of lading are not signed by carrier or its agent or initiated by the party who signed bills of lading.
- "On board" endorsement is not dated.
- Bills of lading are not endorsed.
- Bills of lading are made out "to order" (shipper's order, blank endorsed) where Letter of Credit stipulates "straight" (direct to consignee) bills of adding or vice versa. In some countries, "to order" bills of lading are prohibited and heavy penalties or additional duties are assessed for failure to ship on a "straight" bill of lading.
- Bills of lading are marked "freight prepaid" and freight charges are not included in invoice.
- Description, marks and numbers of merchandise are not the same on all documents presented or are not as required by Letter of Credit.
- Not all documents required by Letter of Credit are presented.
- Documents are "stale dated", that is, not presented within a reasonable time after issuance.
- Invoice does not specify shipment terms (C&F, CIF, FOB, etc.) as stated in Letter of Credit.
- Invoice is not signed as Letter of Credit requires.

Letter of Credit is not cheap to raise and your customer may be reluctant to incur the additional expenditure without some form of "compensation", because your foreign competitors may be offering payment arrangements which are less costly to raise, but, above all, involve them in fewer administrative chores. In simple terms it involves your customer instructing their bank to pay you after a certain period of time, provided all documents are presented to his bank precisely in accordance with all conditions laid down in the Letter of Credit. This substitutes bank risk for buyer risk from the exporter's point of view. The exporter must however present documents, which comply fully with the terms and conditions of the credit.

Letter of Credit is irrevocable, unless specifically stated otherwise, which means that they constitute a definite undertaking and cannot bi revoked or amended without the agreement of all parties.

Direct Interbanking System

This is an interbank payment system whereby funds are collected via a pre-authorized debit on the current account of the debtor. The service is particularly useful where there are regular payments due to the commercial payments or services (e.g. insurance premiums, leasing installments, utilities, etc.)

The procedure, which is completely electronic, enables the creditor, via the bank, to collect at agreed times, funds due, by means of debit being passed to the debtor's account at a bank..

Vocabulary

Reputable *adj.* 声誉好的;受尊敬的;卓越的
having a good reputation

stipulate *v.* 规定;保证
specify as a condition or requirement in a contract or agreement; make an express demand or provision in an agreement; give a guarantee or promise of

subsidiary *n.* 子公司;辅助者
a company that is completely controlled by another company; an assistant subject to the authority or control of another

consign *vt.* 托运;寄存;交付;把……委托给
commit forever; commit irrevocably

reluctant *adj.* 勉强的;不情愿的
unwilling to become involved; not eager

compensation *n.* 补偿;赔偿金;报酬
the act of compensating for service or loss or injury

expenditure *n.* 支出,花费;经费,消费额
the act of spending money for goods or services

substitute *n.* 代替者;代用品; *vi.* 替代,代替

premium *n.* 奖金;保险费,额外费用
a fee charged for exchanging currencies; payment for insurance

exemption *n.* 免除;豁免;免税
immunity from an obligation or duty; a deduction allowed to a taxpayer because of his status

intervention *n.* 介入;妨碍;调停

redeem *v.* 赎回
save from sins

beneficiary *n.* 受益人

applicant *n.* 申请人
irrevocable *adj.* 不可撤销的
amend *v.* 修改
incorporate *v.* 合并,组成公司
make into a whole or make part of a whole
giro *n.* 背书,资金转让
transit *n.* 运输(途中)
neutral *n.* 中性的
stipulated *adj.* 规定的
provisions *n.* 条款
draft *n.* 汇票
drawer *n.* 开票人
drawee *n.* 受票人
viz *adv.* 即,就是
forward *v.* 转交,提交
send or ship onward from an intermediate post or station in transit
reimbursement *n.* 偿还
verify *v.* 核实,查证
confirm the truth of
comply *v.* 顺从,遵守
act in accordance with someone's rules, commands, or wishes
defer *v.* 推迟,延期
circumvent *v.* 规避
avoid or try to avoid fulfilling, answering, or performing (duties, questions, or issues)
authenticity *n.* 真实性,确实性,可靠性
injunction *n.* 禁令,命令
a formal command or admonition
explicitly *adv.* 明确地,明白地
enact *v.* 颁布,制定(法律)
order by virtue of superior authority; decree
discrepancy *n.* 不符合
present *v.* 递交,呈交
waive *v.* 放弃

do without or cease to hold or adhere to
party *n.* 当事人,一方
creditworthiness *n.* 信誉度
scenarios *n.* 情形,情况
justification *n.* 理由
something (such as a fact or circumstance) that shows an action to be reasonable or necessary
fund *v.* 收回资金
misspell *v.* 拼错
expire *v.* 过期
lose validity
instructions *n.* 说明,指示
a manual usually accompanying a technical device and explaining how to install or operate it
inconsistent *adj.* 不一致
displaying a lack of consistency
merchandise *n.* 货物,商品
draft *n.* 汇票
endorse *v.* 背书
countersign *v.* 会签
carrier *n.* 承运人

Phrases

prospective customer	潜在客户
executing a transaction	执行交易
derive from	来源于
comply with	遵守,符合
deferred payment	延期付款
maturity date	到期日
bona fide holders	合法持有人,善意持有人
nominated bank	指定银行
in accordance with	符合,与……一致
draw on	向……开汇票

Chapter 8 Terms of Payment

prior to	在……之前
vice versa	反之亦然

Key terms

terms of payment	付款方式,支付条款
open account	记账(贸易)
letter of credit	信用证
documentary collection	跟单托收
cash against documents	付现交单
bankers draft	银行汇票
issuing bank	开证行
advising bank	通知行
correspondence bank	保兑行
bill of lading	提单
payment undertaking	付款承诺
commercial invoice	商业发票
tenor draft	限期汇票,定期汇票
ports of loading	装运港
ports of destination	目的港
insurance coverage	保险险别
insurance policy	保险单
on board	已装船
to order	抬头为……
freight prepaid	运费预付
freight collect	运费到付
direct interbanking system	直接跨行系统

Post-Reading Activities

I. Answer the following questions based on what you have read in the text.

1. What should be done before agreeing to a method of payment?
2. Why are most foreign trades conducted on an open accounts ?
3. Who are parties to a letter of credit?
4. Why is L/C security for goods and services imported and exported?
5. If discrepancies cannot be corrected or if the discrepancy cannot be corrected within the time stipulated in the Letter of Credit what possible result would the seller be confronted with?

II. Look at the terms in the left-hand column and find the correct definitions in the right-hand column. Copy the corresponding letters in the blanks.

1. _____ draft   A. the exporter delivers all the necessary documents to his own bank which then sends them to a bank in the importer's country. Documents are only released in accordance with the exporter's instructions

2. _____ Documentary Collection   B. a bank or other financial organization that makes credit cards available

3. _____ letter of credit   C. a document issued by a bank that guarantees the payment of a customer's draft; substitutes the bank's credit for the customer's credit

4. _____ Issuing bank   D. a bank in the country of an exporter that tells the exporter about a letter of credit

5. _____ Advising bank   E. a document ordering the payment of money; drawn by one person or bank on another

6. _____ beneficiary   F. a receipt given by the carrier to the shipper acknowledging receipt of the goods being shipped and specifying the terms of delivery

7. _____ bill of lading   G. the recipient of funds or other benefits

III. Translate the following sentences into Chinese.

1. Most of the foreign trade is conducted on an Open Account basis—as the most simple,

straightforward and flexible method available. However you must ensure that your customer is highly reputable, if business is to be conducted on this basis with, for example your invoice being sent direct to them along with documents and requesting payment within the stipulated term.

2. Normally carried out through a bank and a slightly more secure method of trading than Open Account. The exporter delivers all the necessary documents to his own bank which then sends them to a bank in the importer's country. Documents are only released in accordance with the exporter's instructions, e. g. against sight payment, or acceptance of a term Bill of Exchange.

3. Bills of lading are made out "to order" (shipper's order, blank endorsed) where Letter of Credit stipulates "straight" (direct to consignee) bills of adding or vice versa. In some countries, "to order" bills of lading are prohibited and heavy penalties or additional duties are assessed for failure to ship on a "straight" bill of lading.

4. Letter of Credit is irrevocable, unless specifically stated otherwise, which means that they constitute a definite undertaking and cannot be revoked or amended without the agreement of all parties.

5. This is an interbank payment system whereby funds are collected via a pre-authorized debit on the current account of the debtor. The service is particularly useful where there are regular payments due to the commercial payments or services.

IV. Translate the following sentences into English with the words given.

1. 我们同意将即期信用证付款方式改为即期付款交单。(D/P)
2. 对于你方以电汇方式不晚于11月30日预付全部货款,我方表示感谢。(T/T)
3. 为了做成这笔生意,希望双方都各让一步。50%以信用证付款,50%按付款交单,怎么样? (L/C)
4. 很抱歉,贵方订单中规定的付款条件不能为我方所接受。(Terms of Payment)
5. 作为一项特殊照顾,我们接受付款交单方式支付你方这笔试订货。(trial order)

Chapter 9

Transport and Logistics

Pre-reading questions:
1. Do you have an idea about transport?
2. What are logistics services involved?
3. Why is logistics so important?
4. What's the responsibility of the freight forwarder?
5. What's the liability of carrier?

Text

Introduction

Once a company has entered into a sales or purchasing contract with an overseas organization, consideration must be given to the physical transportation of the goods from the point of origin to their final destination. Exporters need to be able to transport their products cost-effectively to their clients and logistics therefore plays an important role in the international trade process.

Logistics system is quite closely related to transportation, as in logistics the movement of goods is a key part. Transportation plays a key role in the logistics system.

The unit aims at providing an insight into the way in which transport intermediaries operate and identifying the issues that must be addressed to ensure that the transportation of goods overseas runs smoothly. It therefore has little bearing on exporters of services such as consultancy, finance and training, which clearly have little call for the transportation of goods. On finishing this unit, the reader will have an understanding of international logistics.

The Ways of Transportation

There are many means of transportation, and each has its advantages and drawbacks. Goods can be transported by a train, a truck, a plane, a ship or through a pipeline. And in recent years, combined transport which is a road-sea-rail carriage appears. The method used depends on time and cost.

1. Land transportation

Land transportation includes railway transportation and truck transportation. Between them, the railway transportation is very important. Railway transportation refers to cargo transportation by train. It is usually used to transport bulk products that are low in value and must travel great distance.

Railway transportation is not affected by weather conditions and is available for cargo transportation all year around. Compared with ocean transportation, it is faster and safer in delivering goods because the risks of damage to the goods are comparatively small.

Compared with railway transportation, road transportation is more flexible as trucks can stop within a city and deliver goods direct to the market. In addition, a truck can start as soon as it is loaded. However, it has limited capacity and relatively high operating cost, the risk of pilferage and damage is also higher. Road transportation is mostly used to transport high-value goods which travel short distances.

We can summarize the features of road transport which go as follows:

● Special distribution ability.

● It is very competitive within certain distance bands compared with air transport both in terms of transport times and rates.

● Documentation is simple. The document used in road transport is the consignment note.

● The service tends to be reliable and to a high standard.

● Packing costs are lower when compared with conventional shipping services.

● The driver accompanies the vehicle throughout the road transit. Therefore, the risk of damage is reduced.

2. Air transportation

Air transport is one of the youngest forms of transport and without doubt, it continues to make a major contribution the exploitation of world resources. The amount of cargo carried by air is very small when compared with the vast bulks carried by sea, but is none the less significant. Air freight is quick although it is expensive. When speed is taken into consideration, this method will be more effective. Food and some urgently needed goods are usually delivered by air freight.

There are many advantages of air transport and the main advantages are stated as below:

● High speed and quick transit.

● Simplified documentation system. One document — an air waybill — is used throughout air freight transit.

● Virtually eliminates packing costs.

● Ideal for a widerange of consumer-type cargoes.

● Service are reliable and to a high quality.

● The air freight network worldwide is more extensive and offers more frequent flights than the maritime services.

Besides the advantages mentioned above, there may be some others.

Although air transport has a number of advantages, it also has some disadvantages which go as follows:

● Limited capacity of air freight and overall dimensions of acceptable cargo together with weight restrictions.

● Cost are higher.

● The service is more easily affected by the weather conditions.

3. Ocean transportation

Ocean transportation has been the most important mode of transport in international trade. Two-thirds of world total volume and over 80% of China's imports and exports are transported by sea. Ocean transport has many advantages. The first advantage is the easy passage since about 70% of the earth is covered by water. Secondly, ocean transport has a large capacity. For example, the deadweight (loaded weight-fuel plus cargo) of the largest oil tanker can be up to 500 000 tons. Thirdly, because of such large capacity, the unit distribution cost is reduced. Of course, there are also disadvantages, one of which is the slow passage of ocean transportation. In addition, ocean transport is also vulnerable to bad weather and less punctual if compared with road or air transport.

4. International multimodal transport

International multimodal transport is the carriage of goods by at least two different modes of transport on the basis of a multimodal transport contract from a place in one country at which the goods are taken in charge by the multimodal transport operator (MTO) to a place designated for delivery situated in a different country.

The Functions of Transportation

1. Bridge over buyer-seller gap

A firm's logistics supply chain is a series of fixed points where the goods come to rest and transportation links. The transportation link makes it possible for goods to flow between the various fixed points and bridges the buyer-seller gap.

2. Value added

Transportation adds value to the firm by creating time and place utility. The value added is the physical movement of goods to the place desired and t the time desired.

3. Global impact

As supply chain become increasingly longer in our global economy, the transportation function is connecting buyers and sellers that may be at the far end of the globe. This wide gap results in greater transportation costs. Besides, much more time is needed in the international transportation. This results in higher inventories and higher storage costs.

4. Cost-service trade-off

For example, if a company switches from rail to air transportation to move raw materials from a vendor to the plant, the air carrier's increased speed, or lower transit time, permits the company to hold lower inventories to meet demand during transit time and to use less warehousing space and less stringent product packaging; but the company realizes these advantages at expenses of higher transportation costs. Thus, a firm cannot make the transportation decision in a vacuum; applying the total cost or systems approach requires a company to consider how the transport decision will affect other elements of the transportation system.

Now we move on to the role and essentials of a logistics.

The Role and Importance of Logistics

Logistics is often perceived as simply the transportation of goods from one place to another. In reality, this definition is too narrow and does not reflect the more complex and comprehensive nature of the function. Logistics is really about managing every aspect of a company's business, from sourcing raw materials to production, warehousing, marketing, pricing, sales and ultimately the transportation of the finished goods to the buyers.

The logistics function begins with an understanding of the requirements of the design and development teams and is used to source components and raw materials quickly and cheaply, either domestically or from around the world. It needs to understand how the product is manufactured in order to take into account any special requirements for packaging, marking and labeling as well as any warehousing considerations.

Logistics is a big business. Its consumption of land, labor, capital, and information — coupled with its impact on the world's standard of living — is enormous. Logistics and the closely related concept of supply chain management are necessary cornerstones of competitive strategy, increased market share, and shareholder's value for most organizations.

The logistics department must then appreciate how the goods have been priced for sale and which delivery terms or other contractually binding clauses have been specified that might have a bearing on transportation. Finally, the logistics manager should be fully aware of where the goods are to be shipped so that the most appropriate method of transport can be identified and arranged.

Logistics is a vital piece of the international trade jigsaw. It is the company's best interest to make effective use of the process and to ensure that costs are kept to minimum wherever possible.

Competitive Advantage of TPL

With the globalization of businesses and the consequent competitive pressures, there has been an increasing dependence on the ability of organizations to deliver customer-adapted products all over the world quickly and on time. This has placed a number of demands on the logistics system and has become a rapidly developing area of investigation. In fact, it has been referred to as the last frontier for the development of strategic competitive advantage. To gain a competitive advantage, many organizations are seeking to manage their logistics operations strategically, but realize that they lack the core competencies and are increasingly seeking to outsource their logistics activities. Apart from this, another important development that is making an impact on the organizations is the increased emphasis on time-based competition. Broadly, time-based competition refers to the speed with which products can be manufactured, delivered to the market and serviced.

The Role of the Freight Forwarder

Freight forwarders are transport intermediaries who are contracted to carry out some or all of the elements of the distribution process. It is within the forwarder's remit to ensure that goods are properly packaged and marked for transport and that appropriate documentation is prepared to facilitate shipment. The freight forwarder can arrange for the integrated transport of consignments. From collection at the exporter's factory and carriage to the point of shipment, to consolidating consignments into a larger, more manageable shipment and booking the required cargo space for the voyage to the target market. On arrival, the forwarder can arrange for the on-carriage of the shipment to the importer, thereby providing a total solution to the exporter's distribution requirements.

Forwarders purchase space on cargo ships/truck/trains/aircraft for particular routes and voyages. The cargo space is generally sold on a Freight All Kinds (FAK) basis, meaning that the forwarder is charged a single rate regardless of the type of goods to be shipped. This space is then resold at a profit by the freight forwarders to their clients at a rate per freight ton or kilogram. As any unsold space must be paid for by the forwarder freight forwarder is therefore a precise operation. No company wants to pay for something that it is not using and freight forwarders consequently become good judges of how much space they are likely to require and be able to sell on. As the forbearers generally do not possess their own vessels, they are normally termed "non-vessel owning common carriers", or NVOCC. The main reason why companies choose to work with freight forwarders is for the cost saving that can be achieved by working with experienced transport organizations that have established their own international contacts within the industry. Although forwarders do charge a fee for their services, this can be built into the pricing equation, provided that appropriate research into transport costs was undertaken prior to the quotation. Freight forwarding is a fiercely competitive industry, with each forwarder offering expertise and strength in different markets. Companies are advised to research potential partners and obtain several quotations for their shipments in order to appoint the most cost-effective and appropriate provider of transport solutions.

Transport Goods without a Freight Forwarder

Even though it is sensible to work with freight forwarders that can use established international networks to identify the most cost-effective means of transporting a consignment to its destination, it is nevertheless possible for companies to dispense with forwarders and arrange shipping themselves. By doing so, the exporter or importer removes the intermediary from the equation and effectively becomes the shipper. Consequently, the company must be prepared to undertake the full range of services normally provided by a forwarder. For this reason, it is not recommended that individual companies make their own shipping arrangements as, in all probability, they will not possess the same level of experience, expertise and contacts as forwarding agents. Companies that nonetheless proceed with contracting for transportation themselves must, as a minimum, address the following issues:

● The ports of origin and destination of the cargo.

● The products to be transported.

● Documentary requirements.

● Rates and terms of payment.

● Liability for injury, loss or damage to cargo, damage to property.

● Performance and penalty clauses.

● Requirements for specific services or equipment to be supplied by the transport company to ensure the safe loading, unloading and storage of the consignment.

● Policy on the replacement value of damaged goods.

● Clause detailing the circumstances under which the contract can be terminated.

● Conditions under which the contract may be altered.

Although the shipper should also ensure that the chosen transport company has the capacity to ship the goods in accordance with its wishes, particularly with regard to the arrangements that the carrier has in place at the ports of origin and destination, as well as the ports through which the vessel will pass on route.

Given the amount of research and preparation that has already gone into the development of the international trade strategy, companies may choose to use the services offered by freight forwarders simply in order to reduce the need for further research. The cost savings generated by cutting out the intermediary may well be negated by the cost of researching transport companies and arranging shipping. Although freight forwarders charge for their services, they do at least have well-established international distribution net work that can be utilized cost-effectively, efficiently and with minimum involvement from the importer or exporter.

Vocabulary

cost-effective *adj.* 有成本效益的,划算的
economical in terms of tangible benefits produced by money spent
client *n.* 顾客,客户
customer
consultancy *n.* 顾问公司,专家咨询
finance *v.* 为……提供资金,融资
to obtain fund or capital
advantage *n.* 优势,优点
a factor or circumstance of benefit to its possessor
drawback *n.* 缺点,弊端
a disadvantage or problem that makes something a less attractive idea
pipeline *n.* 管道
a series of pipes that are usually underground and are used for carrying oil, gas, etc. over long distances
cargo *n.* 货物
the goods carried in a ship or plane
affect *v.* 影响
to make somebody have strong feelings of sadness, pity, etc
available *adj.* 可用的,可得的
that you can get, buy or find
deliver *v.* 交付,送达
to take goods, letters, etc. to the person or people they have been sent to; to take somebody somewhere
pilferage *n.* 偷窃

to steal things of little value or in small quantities, especially from the place where you work

summarize *v.* 总结

to give a summary of something (a statement of the main points)

distribution *n.* 分拨,配送

the act of giving or delivering something to a number of people

competitive *adj.* 有竞争力的,优惠的

as good as or better than others

conventional *adj.* 依照惯例的,约定俗成的,常见的

tending to follow what is done or considered acceptable by society in general; normal and ordinary, and perhaps not very interesting

significant *adj.* 重要的,重大的,显著的,有意义的

large or important enough to have an effect or to be noticed; having a particular meaning

eliminate *v.* 消除,减少

to remove or get rid of something/somebody

urgent *adj.* 紧急的,急迫的

showing that you think that something needs to be dealt with immediately

simplify *v.* 简化,使简易

to make something easier to do or understand

virtually *adv.* 实际上,事实上,差不多

almost or very nearly, so that any slight difference is not important

pack *v.* 包装

to put something into a container so that it can be stored, transported or sold

extensive *adj.* 广泛的,大量的

covering a large area; great in amount

capacity *n.* 容量,容积

the number of things or people that a container or space can hold

dimension *n.* 尺寸,规模

a measurement in space, for example the height, width or length of something

restriction *n.* 限制

a rule or law that limits what you can do or what can happen

bridge *n.* 桥梁

a thing that provides a connection or contact between two different things

     v. 缩短距离

to reduce the distance between widely contrasting groups

gap *n.* 差距,鸿沟

a space between two things or in the middle of something

link *v.* 联系,联结

to connect two things together

    n. 联系,纽带

a connection between two or more people or things

utility *n.* 效用

the quality of being useful

impact *n.* 影响

the powerful effect that something has on somebody/something

inventory *n.* 库存

all the goods in a shop

switch *v.* 转变

to change or make something change from one thing to another

vendor *n.* 摊贩,卖方

a person who sells things, for example food or newspapers, usually outside on the street; a company that sells a particular product

plant *n.* 工厂

a factory or place where power is produced or an industrial process takes place

carrier *n.* 承运人

a company that carries goods or passengers from one place to another

warehouse *n.* 仓库,货栈

a building where large quantities of goods are stored, especially before they are sent to shops/stores to be sold

intermediary *n.* 中间人

person or an organization that helps other people or organizations to make an agreement by being a means of communication between them

remit *n.* 职权范围
the area of activity over which a particular person or group has authority

influence appropriate *adj.* 合适的
suitable, acceptable or correct for the particular circumstances

consequently *adv.* 结果,因此
as a result; therefore

vessel *n.* 船,容器
a large ship or boat; a container

fee *n.* 费,酬金
an amount of money that you pay for professional advice or services

equation *n.* 相等,平衡
the act of making something equal or considering something as equal

fiercely *adv.* 激烈地,猛烈地
strongly

expertise *n.* 专门知识或技能
expert knowledge or skill in a particular subject, activity or jo

quotation *n.* 报价
a statement of how much money a particular goods will cost

consignment *n.* 托运货物
a quantity of goods that are sent or delivered somewhere

penalty *n.* 惩罚,罚金
a punishment for breaking a law, rule or contract

clause *n.* 条款
an item in a legal document that says that a particular thing must or must not be done

terminate *n.* 终结,结束
to end; to make something end

alter *v.* 修改
to change

Phrases

plays an important role in	对……很重要；扮演重要角色
all year around	全年
without doubt	毫无疑问
none the less	依然
take into consideration	把……考虑在内
regardless of	不管，不顾

Key terms

point of origin	起点
final destination	终点
intermediary	中间人
land transportation	陆路运输
air transportation	空运
bulk products	散装货
ocean transportation	海路运输
the risk of pilferage and damage	盗窃和破损险
packing costs	包装成本
the deadweight	最大载重量
international multimodal transport	复合运送人以二种以上的运送方式，将货物由一国境内接管货物的地点运送至另一国境内的指定交付货物的地点
raw materials	原材料
consignment note	托运单
warehousing	仓储
supply chain	供应链管理
delivery terms	交付条款

Third Party Logistics(TPL)	第三方物流
the freight forwarder	货运代理
Freight All Kinds(FAK)	品目无差别运输
Nom-Vessel Owning Common Carriers/NVOCC	无船承运人
the shipper	托运人,发货人

Post-Reading Activities

I. Answer the following questions based on what you have read in the text.

1. Explain the importance of the logistics function in businesses that trade internationally.
2. What are the advantages and disadvantages of air transportation?
3. What's TPL?
4. What are the roles of freight forwarder?

II. Look at the terms in the left-hand column and find the correct definitions in the right-hand column. Copy the corresponding letters in the blanks.

1. _____ freight forwarder
2. _____ Freight All Kinds(FAK)
3. _____ NVOCCs
4. _____ intermediary

A. the crude or processed materials that can be converted by manufacture, processing, or combination into a new and useful product

B. this kind of freight is based on the volume or weight only, and does not consider the attribute, type, and other factors

C. a third party that offers intermediation services between two trading parties

D. it is a company that establishes and maintains its own freight tariff, has the goods shipped in its own name, is responsible for all the transportation and issuing of shipping bill, no matter whether it has or controls the transportation vehicle. It is the carrier for the real owner of the goods, but is the shipper for the shipping company

5. _____ inter-modal transport   E. it is one kind of marine risks that the cargo may be stolen or damaged

6. _____ the risk of theft and damage   F. the firm/person that is entrusted by the owner of goods, go over all the following formalities, declaration, foreign exchange settlement, and inspection, etc. and charge some commission

7. _____ raw material   G. the transport means that the combined transport operator transport the cargo from the place to collect the cargo in one country to the designated place of delivery in another country, using at least 2 kinds of transportation means (railway, maritime and airway, etc.)

III. Translate the following sentences into Chinese.

1. There are many means of transportation, and each has its advantages and drawbacks. Goods can be transported by a train, a truck, a plane, a ship or through a pipeline. And in recent years, combined transport which is a road-sea-rail carriage appears.

2. International multimodal transport is the carriage of goods by at least two different modes of transport on the basis of a multimodal transport contract from a place in one country at which the goods are taken in charge by the multimodal transport operator (MTO) to a place designated for delivery situated in a different country.

3. As supply chain become increasingly longer in our global economy, the transportation function is connecting buyers and sellers that may be at the far end of the globe.

4. Even though it is sensible to work with freight forwarders that can use established international networks to identify the most cost-effective means of transporting a consignment to its destination, it is nevertheless possible for companies to dispense with forwarders and arrange

shipping themselves.

5. Although the shipper should also ensure that the chosen transport company has the capacity to ship the goods in accordance with its wishes, particularly with regard to the arrangements that the carrier has in place at the ports of origin and destination, as well as the ports through which the vessel will pass on route.

IV. Translate the following sentences into English with the words given.

1. 运输在物流系统中起到重要的作用。(play a key role in)
2. 公路运输不受天气状况的影响,可以全年进行货物运输(all year round)
3. 与铁路运输相比,公路运输更加具有灵活性,因为它可以在城市内停留并把货物直接送到市场。(deliver)
4. 物流实际上涉及公司业物的方方面面,从原材料的采购到生产、储存、营销、定价,销售以及最终把产成品交付到顾客手里。(warehouse)
5. 在公路运输中所使用的单据叫托运单。(consignment note)

Chapter 10

Meeting People

Background Briefing

In the business world there is a saying, "no customer, no business." In order to do excellent international trading work it is necessary to keep good communications with others. The importer and the exporter will find some channels of the perfect understanding between each other as following: attendance at the export commodities fairs, contact at exhibitions held at home and abroad, mutual visits by trademen, introduction from friends or other business connections and groups.

During the business activities, it is common for trademen from different counties to meet and introduce eath other in English. Business greeting is a way of being friendly to someone and also a way of starting a conversation. Another important point is different customs and habits between China and the English-speaking countries.

Situational Conversation

Dailogue A

Making New Contact at the Canton Fair

Situation: Lin Lan, the sales manager of Rainbow Import & Export co. is invited to the Canton fair. She hope to improve her business with orders from the fair. Now she is seeking new dealers at the Exhibition Hall.

(L:Lin   D:David)

L: Good morning, sir. This is Rainbow Import & Export Co. I'm Lin Lan. Can I help you?

D: Nice to meet you, Lin Lan. I'm David Brown. This is my business card.

L: Nice to meet you too, Mr. Brown. Here is my name card. May I ask what line of business you are in?

D: I'm in textiles.

L: I see. Our textiles have won great popularity in the world. We have many years' experience and professional knowledge in the foreign trade and have established trade relations with other countries like European countries, the United States, South Korea, Singapore and Japan. Here is our product information sheet. On the display are some of the samples. Wish you have interests.

D: Nice to know you, Miss Lin. Surely we are looking for suppliers of the cotton embroidered dresses recently.

L: Great. We can surely meet your demand. We are one of the leading exporters of the cotton embroidered dresses in China.

D: We are one of the most powerful wholesalers of the cotton embroidered dresses in U.S.A. We wish to market the goods on the basis of equality and mutual benefit in the future.

L: The same idea. We can assure you that the product we supplied is superb quality, and the price is the most favorable. The sufficient supplies and on-time delivery are also guaranteed.

D: Wonderful! We should negotiate more details further. I will visit your company ASAP.

L: Contact me at any time. We will arrange for your coming.

D: Thank you. Keep in touch. Goodbye.

Dialogue B

Welcoming the Guest at the Airport

Situation: Susan Wang, general manager of Rainbow Import & Export co. and her secretary, Diana Liu are going to meet Fred Johns, the purchase manager of Global Trading Inc at Beijing International Airport.

(L: Liu   J: Johns   W: Wang)

L: Excuse me, sir. Are you Mr. Johns from Global Trading Inc., New York?

J: Yes, I am. You must be Diana Liu from Rainbow Import & Export co.?

L: Yes, it's my pleasure to meet you. Welcome to Beijing. Did you have a pleasant trip?

J: Well, I enjoyed it very much.

L: Anyway it's a long way to China, isn't it? I think you must be very tired.

J: But I will be all right by tomorrow, and ready for business.

L: I would like to introduce you to Miss Wang, our general manager. Miss Wang, this is Mr.

Johns, the purchase manager from Global Trading Inc.

J: Nice to meet you, Miss Wang.

W: Nice to meet you, Mr. Johns. Welcome to our city. I hope you will enjoy your stay here.

J: Thank you. I have been looking forward to this trip.

W: We'll do everything we can to accommodate you and make you comfortable.

J: You are so nice. I hope we'll have a good cooperation.

W: Great. Now let's take a short rest in the waiting room. Then Miss Liu and I will take you to visit our company.

J: Good idea. Let's go.

Dialogue C

Receiving the Client at Office

Situation: Mr. Johns arrives at the office, then Miss Wang and Mr. chen are introducing the company to him.

(C: Chen   J: Johns   W: Wang)

W: Here is our company, Rainbow Import & Export co. .

J: Yes, I've heard the company for a long time.

W: Well, we have been in this line for a long time. And we are one of the most competitive suppliers of this line. We have nearly 280 employees and sales of $ 806 million. We manufacture fine textiles, e. g the cotton embroidered dresses. Our products are sold in Britain, America, Japan, Italy and South East Asia and well appreciated by their purchasers.

C: Yes, and we always take customers first.

J: Great. Do you have any new products?

W: Yes, it is researched by our Research and Development Department. I think it will be the best-seller.

J: Wonderful.

W: Miss Li will show you around the different departments of our country.

C: Follow me please, Mr. Johns. This is our marketing department.

J: Looks great.

C: Yes, Marketing department mainly advertises and markets products. And this way, this is our Research and Development department.

J: I've heard a new kind of textiles has been developed by this department.

C: Yes, this department is very important for the company. It is called "heart" of the company.

J: Do you have Dispatch department?

C: Of course, please turn right, and this is our Dispatch Department, which is responsible to send goods to customers. And we have a great After-sales department.

J: It means whatever problems we have after sales, we can get help from this department.

C: Yes, we always take customers as our Gods. Our after-sales service is perfect.

J: That's great. Thank you.

C: Ok, let's go to my office and have a cup of tea.

Vocabulary

contact *n.* 接触,联系
exhibition *n.* 展览,展示;展览会
import: *n.* 进口,输入;进口商品
export *n.* 出口,输出;出口商品
line *n.* 行业
textile *n.* 纺织品;(pl) textiles *n.* 纺织品;纺织业
relationship *n.* 关联;关系(＝relation)
embroider *v.* 绣花;刺绣(*n.* embroidery)
equality *n.* 平等;相等;同等,等同性
mutual *adj.* 相互的,彼此的;共同的
professional *adj.* 职业的;专业的;*n.* 专业人员;内行
assure＝make sure
guarantee *v.* 保证;担保
accommodate *v.* 向……提供住处,提供住宿
cooperation *n.* 合作,协作
competitive *adj.* 竞争的,比赛的
supplier *n.* 供应商
appreciate *v.* 欣赏,感激,赏识
purchaser *n.* 买方,购买者

Phrases

sales manager	销售经理
professional knowledge	专业知识
establish trade relations with sb.	与某人建立贸易关系
product information sheet	产品说明书
on the basis of	在……的基础上
in detail	详细地
meet one's demand	满足某人的要求,也可以用 meet one's needs
leading exporters	主要出口商
ASAP = as soon as possible	尽快
assure sb. of sth.	向某人保证某事
assure sb. that...	向某人保证……
be interested in...	对……感兴趣
make sb. comfortable	使某人宾至如归
hear... for a long time	久仰大名
Global Trading Inc.	Inc=incorporation 公司 全球贸易公司
Research and Development Department	研究和发展部门
the best-seller	畅销品
marketing department	市场部门
dispatch department	运输部门
after-sales department	售后服务部门

Useful Sentences

1. What line of business you are in?
   你做哪一行?
2. I'd like to establish trade relations with you.
   我想与贵方建立业务关系。
3. Wish you have interests.
   希望你感兴趣。

4. Could you explain it in detail?
   你能说得详细些吗?

5. We can surely meet your demand.
   我们肯定可以满足你方的需求。

6. We can assure you that the product we supplied is superb quality, and the price is the most favorable.
   我们能保证我们的产品不仅质量好而且价格是最优惠的。
   We assure you of the qulity.
   我们保证货的质量。
   We assure you that you are mistaken.
   我肯定地说你弄错了。

7. The sufficient supplies and on-time delivery are also guaranteed.
   保证货源充足交货及时。

8. Please reply as soon as possible.
   请尽快答复。

9. Contact me at any time.
   随时跟我联系。

10. Let me introduce you to Mr. Li, general manager of our company.
    让我介绍你认识,这是我们的总经理,李先生。

11. We'll do everything we can to accommodate you and make you comfortable.
    我们会尽力为您服务,使您有一种舒适如归的感觉。

Related Sentences

I. Greeting (formal)

1. Pleased to meet you, Mr. Smith.　　很高兴见到你,史密斯先生。
2. How are you doing?　　你怎么样?
3. Glad to meet you here.　　很高兴在这里见到你。
4. Good to see you again.　　很高兴又见到你。
5. How nice to see you.　　见到你真高兴。
6. How is everything? /How is it going? /What's up? /What's new? /How goes it? /What's with you?

Chapter 10 Meeting People

Responses

1. Very well, thank you. 很好,谢谢。
2. Fine, thank you. And you? 很好,谢谢。你呢?
3. Nice/Glad/Pleased to meet/see you, too. 我也很高兴见到你。

Responses

1. Fine, just fine. 不错,还行。
2. Just so so, thanks. 马马虎虎,谢谢。
3. Can't complain. 还过得去。
4. Not too bad, thanks. 还可以,谢谢。
5. Not too much. 不怎么样。
6. Same as ever. 同以前一样。
7. About the same. 差不多吧。
8. Couldn't be better/worse! 非常好(非常糟糕)。
9. Good, I'm on the top of the world! 太好了。
10. Can't complain, I'm still alive. 凑合吧,还活着呢。
11. Pretty bad/awful. 非常不好。

Greeting(informal)

1. It's a long time since we parted. 我们上次见面到现在已经很久了。
   简写 Long time no see. 很久没见了。
2. I haven't seen you for a long time. 很久没见到你了。
3. Fancy seeing you here. 真想不到在这儿遇到你。
4. Good day, mate. 你好,伙计(澳大利亚口语)
5. Haven't seen you for ages. 好久不见了。
6. Hi, buddy! Small world, isn't it? 你好,老兄! 又见面了。
7. What brings you here today? 今天什么风把你吹来啦?

II. Self-introduction

1. I'm Li Ming from Harbin Mechanical Imp. & Exp. Corporation.
   我是哈尔滨机械进出口公司的李明。
2. My name is Zhang Li, from Xinghai International Co. Ltd.
   我叫张力,是星海国际有限公司的。
3. Let me introduce myself. I'm Liu Jun from the Global Trading Company.

让我自我介绍一下。我是全球贸易公司的刘君。

III. Introducing others

1. Michael, may I introduce you to my secretary, Miss. Li?
   迈克尔,请允许我向你介绍我的秘书,李小姐。
2. Allow me to introduce Mr. Wang, the vice-president of our company.
   请允许我介绍一下王先生,我们公司的副总。
3. I'd like to introduce you to Mr. Song.
   我想介绍你给宋先生认识。
4. Please let me introduce Mr. Ross, head of the Market Department.
   请允许我介绍一下市场部主任罗斯先生。

Responses

1. It's a pleasure to know you. 很高兴认识你。
2. I'm pleased to make your acquaintance. 很高兴认识你。
3. Nice/delighted/glad/happy to meet you. 很高兴认识你。

IV. Introducing a company

1. We're one of the leading importers of sportswear in Indonesia.
   我们是印度尼西亚运动服装的主要进口商之一。
2. We've been in this line of business for more than twenty years.
   我们做这一行已有 20 多年了。
3. We are exporters/importers of machine tools.
   我们是机床出口商/进口商。
4. We have been exporting silks for more than ten years.
   我们经营丝绸出口已有 10 多年了。
5. We are very experienced in the freight forwarding agency.
   我们在货运代理业务方面很有经验。

Tip

The Canton Fair: it refers to The China Import and Export Fair, it is a trade fair held in the spring and autumn seasons each year since the spring of 1957 in Canton, Among China's largest trade fairs, it has the largest assortment of products, the largest attendance, and the largest number of business deals made at the fair.

Exercises

I. Complete the Following Dialogues.

1. A: Good morning, sir.
   B: Good morning, _____.(我是来自海外贸易公司的大卫)
   A: Welcome, I'm Mary. _____.(这是我的名片) What can I do for you?
   B: I got the news from my friend that your product are well-received in our country, _____.(我对你们公司的化工产品感兴趣)
   A: Well, _____.(谢谢你的关注)
   B: Can you tell me something about your new products?
   A: Sure, I highly recommend to you our newly developed ones. _____.(这是我们的产品目录和价格表。)
   A: Great! _____?(这些包含了你所有产品吗?)
   B: Yes. _____.(如果你有兴趣,请告诉我)
   A: Thank you very much.

2. A: _____.(我们从中国日报获知贵公司的名称和地址)We noted you are interested in importing Chinese Cotton Piece Goods. _____.(我们想要与你公司建立贸易关系)
   B: We are one of the largest import and export companies in Turkey. _____.(我们进口中国棉布商品好几年了)
   A: _____.(这是我们的产品说明书)Wish you would have interests. _____.(跟其他供应商的货物相比,我们公司的产品价廉物美)
   B: If your conditions are favorable, we'll _____.(安排进一步的会谈)
   A: That'll be fine.

3. A: You must be tired. Mr. Green. Sit here and have a short rest, please.
   B: _____.(谢谢,张小姐。你来接我真是太好了。我感到有点儿累,但我想很快就会恢复的。)

4. A: I do hope you have a pleasant trip.
   B: _____.(总的说来不坏,这天气正好适合旅行。)

5. A: I am sorry for troubling you so much, Miss Zhao.

B:_____.(没关系,我很乐意帮忙。)

6. A:Do you think Mr. White could see me next Monday?

B:_____.(如果一切顺利的话,他要下午三点钟才回来。我们下午的办公时间是2:30-6:00。我们把时间定在三点行吗?)

7. A:Will it be convenient if I call on your manager at 4 o'clock this afternoon?

B:_____.(恐怕有点问题,今天下午4点种他已经有约会了。我们把时间推迟到明天上午8点行吗?那时他有空。)

8. A:Shall we appoint a place to meet this evening?

B:_____.(对不起,我安排不了,今晚我有客人来,我们得把约会推迟一点。)

9. A:About our appointment for the next Monday morning, I wonder whether we could change it from 8:00 to 10:00, because something has come up.

B:_____.(没关系,我们把见面时间改到下周二上午十点钟,在会议室。)

10. A:Hi, Mr. Smith, the Guangzhou Spring Trade Fair is to open tomorrow morning. Would you like to go there for a visit?

B:_____.(妙极了,我想去参观下,和中国商人做几笔大买卖。)

11. A:This is Miss Wang, your interpreter and guide. She will introduce the products displayed in the hall to you.

B:_____.(哦,王小姐,见到你我很高兴,我叫保罗·高曼。这是我的名片,请你简单地向我介绍一下展览会的情况好吗?)

12. A:Many Chinese foreign corporations come to the Fair and do both import and export business.

B:_____.(我想,这是和他们洽谈生意的好机会,大笔买卖将在展览会上做成。)

II. Make a dialogue according to the following information.

(1)联系业务

A:布莱克先生,您好吗?

B:我很好,谢谢.您好吗?

A:非常好,谢谢您。很高兴在这儿遇见您。生意怎么样?

B:相当好,最近市场很繁荣。

A:我希望我们能一起做更多的生意,我们之间建立业务关系对双方有益。

B:我也希望如此. 鉴于对过去的贸易业绩记录满意,我们有可能在更多的业务上进行合作。

(2) 接机
A:对不起,请问你是来自美国的怀特先生吗?
B:是的,我是来自洛杉矶克拉克·怀特,您一定是李小姐。
A:是的,我是来自上海进出口公司的李兰。
B:你好,非常感谢你来接我。
A:您太客气了。旅途如何?
B:很好。全程都很舒服。

(3) 参观部门
A:您好,怀特先生,很荣幸为你介绍我公司的部门。请跟我走。
B:多谢你,李小姐。
A:这里是研发部门,这是我们最重要的部门之一,负责新产品的开发与研究。
B:很好。请问哪里是市场部门。贵公司的市场策略做得很好。
A:多谢您的夸奖。到二楼,右转,就是市场部。参观完市场部以后,我们就要去售后服务部门。
B:作为顾客,我们对你方的售后服务很关注。
A:请放心。我们一贯把顾客看做是上帝,我们的售后服务是优良的。

(4) 拜访经理
A:早上好,先生。请问有什么可以帮忙的吗?
B:是的,我和你们的经理王先生有约。
A:请问您的名字是?
B:我是来自美国的克拉克·怀特。
A:谢谢,怀特先生。我给王先生办公室打个电话(电话中)。王先生办公室? 这里是接待处。怀特先生说与您有约。
C:请他进来。
A:谢谢。(对怀特先生)王先生正等着您。请坐电梯到三楼。然后右转。王先生的办公室在308。
B:非常感谢。
A:没关系。

III. Group Work .

Situational Practice

1. You are from Sunshine Arts and Crafts Ltd. Mr. King, who is from New Century Trading Company in London gets your information from the Internet, www. alibaba. com. He comes to your booth at the trade show to seek the possibility of establishing trade relations with you. Since it is the first time for you to do business with Mr. King, you'd like to know more about his company's financial position, credit standing and trade reputation. Therefore, you ask him to tell you his regular bank so that you could acquaint with his company.

2. You sell trainers on behalf of Global International Company. You meet your old customer Mr. Brown, a wholesaler from Brothers Company in Australia at the trade fair. You are satisfied with your past trade record. You'd like to do more business with him.

Chapter 11

Product Presentation

Warm-up Exercise

1. Translate the following passage into Chinese

Product presentations are an important part of selling your product to prospective customers. In many cases, this will be the customer's first introduction to your company. First impressions are critical. There are also times when it is important to sell your product to the people inside your company as well as investors. Proper preparation is vital to presenting your product in the best light possible.

The objective of the product presentation is different depending upon the target audience and the presentation should be adjusted accordingly. It is important to know your audience and why they are interested enough to hear your presentation.

Points to Consider

Before you even start building your presentation, be sure you know the following information:

Objective/call to action—At the end of your product presentation you want something to happen, either you want a customer to move forward to evaluate your product, your management to buy into what you are doing with the product, your sales people eager to sell your product, or an investor or your management to provide additional funding of your product.

Target audience—Who are you giving the presentation to? (Prospective customers, investors, management) What is their industry like right now? What are their needs and immediate concerns?

What are their individual goals? Where is their pain?

Orientation—How much does your audience know of your product and other similar products? What is special about the way this audience looks at your product? Do they have any preconceived notions? Are they looking at competitors? If so, which ones? What are their special interests?

Target presenter—Who will be giving the presentation (you, sales person, company executive)?

It is helpful to write the above information down before building the product presentation so that you can go back and review it if you get stuck on any given point. You will want to refer to it later to make sure the presentation meets the objective and you will also need it for doing practice runs.

Once you have your basic product presentation, it can be modified for other presenters and other audiences, but it is important to have a target audience and a target objective when building the initial presentation. Failure to do so can result in a presentation that doesn't speak to the audience and one that is not focused on their needs.

2. Which of the followings should be included in a product presentation checklist?

Identify Objective	( )
Identify Target Audience	( )
Identify the Point of the Presentation	( )
Include Positioning	( )
Include Company Overview	( )
Include Product Description	( )
Include Benefits	( )
Include Examples	( )
Indentify and Include Closing Argument	( )

Sample Dialogue & Monologue

Dialogue 1

A: Good morning, sir. Welcome to our shop. Is there anything I can do for you?

B: Good morning. I'd like to buy a photocopier.

A: Would you like to have a look at our photocopiers on show first?

B: Yes, thank you. Well, this one looks nice. Can you tell me about this model?

A: Yes, of course. This model is our latest product. It was launched this summer. As you can see, it has an attractive shape. Compared with other products, it is relatively small in size and light in weight. It only weights 9 kilograms. Its width, depth and height is 33.3 cm, 56.6 cm, 35.8 cm respectively. This model has three colors available: white, gray and green.

B: How many sheets of paper can it copy a minute?

A: It can make 100 copies a minute. It's quite fast, isn't it? What's more, this model makes little noise while in operation. And you will also find it easy to operate.

B: Would you please give me a demonstration?

A: Sure.

B: (After the demonstration) Oh, it's very convenient. Well, what is worrying me is its after-sales service.

A: I can assure you of its quality. This model is very sophisticated in technology, and therefore, needs little maintenance. We offer you a two-year warranty. Besides, we provide free on-site maintenance. If there's something wrong with the machine, just contact us. We'll send a technician over as soon as possible.

B: How much is it?

A: We charge 12 000 Yuan for each copier. I think this price is quite reasonable, compared with other products in terms of performance and quality.

B: OK. I'll take this model, in gray. I hope you can deliver it to our company today.

A: No problem.

Dialogue 2

(Martin is introducing a new product to John...)

Martin: I want to show you something incredible. This is an amazing new product, John. It's a revolutionary product!

John: Is it a computer?

Martin: No, John. It isn't a computer, it's an automatic electronic secretary.

John: Gosh! What does it do?

Martin: It answers the phone. It types letters. It does everything.

John: Gee! Can you show me?

Martin: Yes, John, certainly! What's the name of your company, John?

John: Plastic Box.

Martin: OK...Listen to this!

Computer Secretary: Good morning, Plastic Box Company. This is John Berry's secretary. Can I help you?

Martin: Yes...And if you're not in the office.

Computer Secretary: Good morning. John Berry's secretary here. I'm sorry, Mr Berry isn't in the office this morning. Can I take a message?

John: Gee, she's beautiful. I want to buy her!

Martin: Fine! Can you sign here, please?

John: There you are!

Martin: Thank you very much, John. See you again!

John: Good Bye!

Monologue

(Mr. Harmer, a project manager is presenting a product to his distributors.)

Thank you for giving me the opportunity to present you the latest model of our mobile phone — Sweetvoice 2008. I intend to briefly run through the 3 P's for the new model — the product, the place and the price. Please feel free to interrupt me wherever you've got a question.

To start with, I'll focus on the features of this new model. If you look at the screen behind me showing a picture of Sweetvoice 2008 and the animation of its functions, you'll see that it is small enough to fit right into the palm of your hand. It has a decent weight and an internal antenna. The phone includes a WAP browser so you can connect to the Internet, as well as SIM based information services. There is a 100-name internal phone book in addition to those that you can store on the SIM card, and there is a space for up to 12 voice dialing slots, which serves as the selling point of this model. The 2008 model comes with 38 ring tones, with space for 9 more downloading the ring tones from the Internet, plus a ring tone composer. A vibrating alert discreetly informs you of the incoming calls and messages, while five games will stop you from getting bored. Of course, it has all those common features such as clock, alarm, reminders, stopwatch, countdown timer, calculator, currency converter, etc. I hope that all make sense. In any case, I'll leave these written specifications with you, which you can study at your leisure.

OK, now let me move on to the next point, the place. By place, I mean how we are going to distribute the product and where. The launch date for the Sweetvoice 2008 will be January 1 next year since it will definitely be a season to buy new mobile phones as presents for New Year or the Spring Festival. It will then be in stock in all registered retail outlets throughout the country. We will also be making the phone available by mail order and online order with a guaranteed 6 days delivery.

Pricing comes along with the product going on the market. At present, the new model will retail at approximately 3 000 Yuan. It should be quite a reasonable price concerning the quality and the advanced features.

Right, I'll stop here. I hope you have a clearer picture of the new model—Sweetvoice 2008. I'm also sure that you now share my enthusiasm for the product and hopefully you will be 100% satisfied with this model. Thank you for you time and attention.

Useful Expressions

1. Talking about specifications and sizes

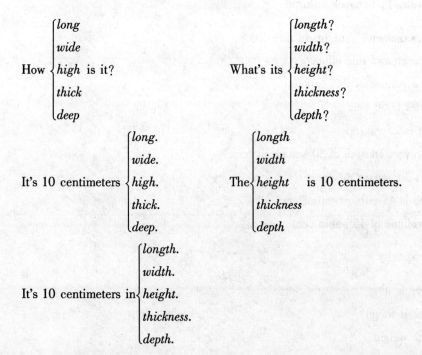

Notes

A. Generally, we use "high" for measurements of most things; we use "tall" for people, buildings and ships, e.g.

My brother is very tall; he is two meters tall.

That's tall building.

That fax machine is only 18 cm high.

B. When we describe the dimensions of an object, we seldom use "dimension" words. We just say "by":

15×8×10cm—fifteen by eight by ten centimeters

C. We can also ask about measurements, dimensions or specifications like this:

What are its measurements, dimensions or specifications?

We have a complete range of specifications.

How big is it?

What size is it?

2. Diameter (radius), area or volume

(1) What's the diameter / radius of this disk?

(2) What's the area of this office?

(3) What's the volume of this container?

(4) Its diameter is 50 cm.

(5) Its radius is 25 cm.

(6) It has / covers an area of 30 square meters.

(7) Its area is 30 square meters.

(8) Its volume is 45 cubic centimeters.

(9) It has a volume of 45 cubic centimeters.

3. Weight and capacity

(1) How heavy is it?

(2) What does it weigh?

(3) What's the weight?

(4) How much can it carry / hold?

(5) What's its maximum load?

(6) It weighs 10 kilograms.

(7) The weight is 10 kilograms.

(8) It can hold / carry 5 000 kg.

4. Shapes, colors and materials

(1) What is the shape of this product?

(2) What's its shape?

(3) What does it look like?

(4) What color is it?

(5) How many colors does it come in?

(6) What's it made of / form?

(7) It has the shape of an apple.

(8) It is shaped like a hook.

(9) It is round / pear-shaped.

(10) It looks like a pyramid.

(11) It is red / light blue.

(12) It comes in three colors: white, black and gray.

(13) It's made of steel. / The paper is made from wood.

Notes

A. We use "light / pale" or "dark / deep" to distinguish the shades of color.

B. "Be made of" and "be made from" have very similar meanings. But often we use "be made of" when the original material can be recognized. We use "be made from" when the original material has been completely changed.

C. We use the following expressions to show the origin of a product, e. g.

The cars are made in Japan.

In Shanghai you can see many cars of German make.

5. Comparing products

(1) Compared with competing products, ours look better and are lower in price.
(2) This computer runs faster than that one.
(3) Our product is the best-selling model of its kind.

6. Include feature, function and benefit in your product presentation

	FEATURE What is it...	FUNCTION What does it do...	BENEFIT For the Customer...
1	The tub in this washer is made of stainless steel.	SO THAT the surface of the tub is perfectly smooth, and it will never rust or corrode.	WHICH MEANS YOUR clothing will last longer, and you'll never have to replace the tub. In any case you'll save money.
2	This dishwasher has its silverware basket in the door.	SO THAT you eliminate the danger of sharp knives and forks pointing up, as in most other brands.	WHICH MEANS YOU will avoid the possibility of a serious injury to yourself or a member of your family.
3	This video recorder records at three different speeds.	SO THAT you may record at a slow, fast or extra fast speed.	WHICH MEANS YOU record in the most economical speed or to record the best picture possible.
4	This sofa has a kiln dried hardwood frame.	SO THAT the frame will never twist, bow or warp.	WHICH MEANS YOUR new sofa will remain comfortable and look new longer.

Vocabulary

audience *n.* 观众,听众
orientation *n.* 定位
photocopier *n.* 复印机
kilogram *n.* 千克
demonstration *n.* 演示
convenient *adj.* 方便的,便利的
sophisticated *adj.* 复杂的;精致的,圆滑的
maintenance *n.* 维修,维护
technician *n.* 技术人员
incredible *adj.* 难以置信的
amazing *adj.* 令人惊异的
revolutionary *adj.* 革命性的
automatic *adj.* 自动的
animation *n.* 动画
browser *n.* 浏览器
discreetly *adv.* 谨慎地,小心地
reminders *n.* 备忘录
stopwatch *n.* 秒表
calculator *n.* 计算器
specifications *n.* 技术规格
enthusiasm *n.* 热情

Key terms

product presentation	产品介绍
after-sales service	售后服务
on-site maintenance	现场维修
selling point	卖点
ring tones	手机铃声
countdown timer	倒数计时器
currency converter	货币换算

Exercises

1. Choose one product from the following pictures and demonstrate the product presentation

2. Work in pairs. Let the Ss describe one of the pictures with their partners.

3. Supplementary Reading

Outline of the Product Presentation

The following is a basic outline for a product presentation. You will note that the maximum number of slides is twenty. Most sales calls allow 30 minutes for the formal presentation, at two minutes a slide, fifteen slides is the appropriate number. It is important to keep your presentation precise otherwise your point will be drowned out in detail.

(1) Introduction—This is normally just a title slide where the speaker introduces themselves, and the point of the product presentation. This is where you want to hook your audience and tell them what is in it for them. If you are not going to be giving the presentation you may want to have a note slide with the point on it. (1—2 slides)

(2) Agenda—An agenda is optional, but provides you with an your opportunity to tell your audience what you are going to cover in your presentation. It avoids people asking questions early in the presentation about material you will be covering later. (1 slide)

(3) Company Information—This is a way to establish credibility and to make the audience feel comfortable with your company. Ways to do this include customer lists, high-profile executives or advisors, information on funding (if a private company), awards and major milestones. Don't spend too much time on this, you don't want your audience falling asleep. In fact, in my more recent presentations I have moved this to the back, after I have the audience's attention.

(4) Positioning—Successful products have a unique technology or positioning that sets them apart from other products on the market. You want to introduce this aspect of your product up front to let your audience know how your product is different and why they should listen to the rest of your presentation. Use this as an attention getter. This should be done in terms of the problem that they have and that you are solving with your product. Be sure to present this in terms of your audience and their pain. Performing a positioning exercise prior to building your presentation is very helpful. This part of your presentation must be very crisp and to the point. (1—5 slides)

(5) Product description—Clearly describe your product in terms that your audience will understand. It may be helpful to have a chart with the product components. You want to give the audience a frame of reference for the features and benefits that they are going to see. You also want them to know how your product fits into their existing environment. Show how the product interfaces with other products or systems they may be using. (1—2 slides)

(6) Clearly articulated benefits as they relate to your target audience—You can use a features and benefits list or just walk through the features and benefits. Whatever you do, do not forget the benefits! They may be obvious to you because you live and breath the product, but your audience should have them clearly called out and they must relate to their needs. (1—5 slides)

(7) Examples/successes—At this point in the presentation your audience should be familiar with your product and why it is different and better. In order to drive this point home use examples of how your product is being used and how customers have benefited from the product. (1—3

slides)

(8) Closing argument—This is your opportunity for a "call to action". You want summarize your product presentation, reiterate the point of the presentation, and ask your audience to do something, if that is the point of your presentation.

When You are the Presenter

Practice your presentation. No one ever has the time to do it, but even if you are used to winging presentations, the following are the benefits of practice:

(1) Your pitch will be more powerful, polished, and professional

(2) You are more likely to accomplish your objective

(3) You look better

There is nothing worse then watching a presenter bring up a slide and then try to interpret it as if this is the first time they are seeing it. The slides are to support your presentation. I will often give the presentation to a practice audience within the company first before giving it to an external audience. You will get some great suggestions from people who have a slightly different perspective. This is especially true if you can give your pitch to a different department. I have found that giving a product presentation to the engineering group will provide some great insights. Before you give your presentation to a practice audience, be sure to go over the "Points to Consider" above with your audience so that they understand your objective, target audience, and that target audience's perspective.

Additionally you should add slides that talk specifically to your audience. Identify the issues and problems that they are dealing with or tell them about how their competition is doing something. Then show them how your product will provide them with a competitive advantage.

Chapter 12

Business Dinner

Warm-up Exercise

1. Business and social etiquette can be tricky, and making the right moves can make a big difference. Take this quick quiz and see how you fare in the following business situations.

(1) Your boss, Ms. Alpha, enters the room when you're meeting with an important client, Mr. Beta. You stand up and say "Ms. Alpha, I'd like you to meet Mr. Beta, our client from San Diego."

(2) You're entering a cab with an important client. You position yourself so the client is seated curbside. Is this correct?

(3) A toast has been proposed in your honor. You say "thank you" and take a sip of your drink. Are you correct?

(4) You're at a table in a restaurant for a business dinner. Midway through the meal, you're called to the telephone. What do you do with your napkin?

(5) You're greeting or saying good-bye to someone. When's the proper time to shake their hand?

(6) You've forgotten a lunch with a business associate. You feel terrible and know he's furious. What should you do?

(7) You're in a restaurant and a thin soup is served in a cup with no handles. To eat it you should:

    A. pick it up and drink it.

    B. use the spoon provided.

C. eat half of it with a spoon and drink the remainder.

(8) You're at a dinner and champagne is served with the dessert. You simply can't drink champagne yet know the host will be offering a toast. Do you:

A. tell the waiter "no champagne"?

B. turn over your glass?

C. ask the waiter to pour water into your champagne glass instead?

D. say nothing and allow the champagne to be poured?

(9) You're at a table in a restaurant for a business dinner. Midway through the meal, you're called to the telephone. What do you do with your napkin?

A. Take it with you.

B. Fold and place it to the left of your plate.

C. Loosely fold it and place it on the right side.

D. Leave it on your chair.

(10) You're hosting a dinner party at a restaurant. Included are two other couples, and your most valuable client and his wife. You instruct the waiter to:

A. serve your spouse first.

B. serve your client's spouse first.

C. serve you and your spouse last.

(11) You're invited to a reception and the invitation states "7:00 to 9:00 P. M." You should arrive:

A. at 7:00 P. M..

B. anytime between 7:00 P. M. and 9:00 P. M..

C. between 7:00 P. M. and 7:30 P. M..

D. go early and leave early.

(12) You're greeting or saying good-bye to someone. When's the proper time to shake their hand?

A. When you're introduced.

B. At their home.

C. At their office.

D. On the street.

E. When you say good-bye.

(13) You're talking with a group of four people. Do you make eye contact with:

A. just the person to whom you're speaking at the moment?

B. each of the four, moving your eye contact from one to another?

C. no one particular person (not looking directly into anyone's eyes)?

(14) The waiter's coming toward you to serve wine. You don't want any. You turn your glass upside down. Are you correct?

(15) when you greet a visitor in your office, do you:

A. say nothing and let her sit where she wishes?

B. tell her where to sit?

C. say "Just sit anywhere"

(16) You're invited to dinner in a private home. When do you take your napkin from the table and place it on your lap?

A. Open it immediately.

B. Wait for the host to take his napkin before taking yours.

C. Wait for the oldest person at the table to take his.

D. Wait for the acknowledged head of the table to take hers before taking yours.

(17) You're scheduled to meet a business associate for working lunch and you arrive a few minutes early to find a suitable table. 30 minutes later your associate still hasn't arrived. Do you:

A. order your lunch and eat?

B. continue waiting and fuming that your associate isn't there?

C. tell the head waiter you're not staying and give him our card with instructions to present it to your associate to prove you were there?

D. after 15 minutes call your associate?

(18) You've forgotten a lunch with a business associate. You feel terrible and know he's furious. Do you:

A. write a letter of apology?

B. send flowers?

C. keep quiet and hope he forgets about it?

D. call and set up another appointment?

2. Can you say the following tableware in English, and how to use them?

Sample Dialogues

Dialogue 1　Making Reservation

(A: attendant　B: Mr. Smith)

A: Good morning, sir. Can I help you?

B: Good morning. I'd like to reserve a private room for a banquet here.

A: Certainly. How many people?

B: Will, let me see. I have invited eleven Chinese friends. Including myself, altogether twelve.

A: So you would need one table for twelve people in a private room.

B: Can you tell me the name of the room now?

A: Please wait a moment. We will arrange the room "Mudan" for you.

B: By the way, is Mudan equipped with Karaokay equipment? You see my Chinese friends like Karaokay very much.

A: Oh sorry. Room Mudan can't be used for karaokay.

B: Is it possible to change a room with karaokay equipment?

· 155 ·

A: Let me check whether there are any vacant rooms. How about Room Yueji? It's at the end of the third floor. The rooms on the second floor are all booked. Does it matter?

B: It doesn't matter.

A: When will you come?

B: About 6:30 p.m.

A: Would you mind leaving your name and telephone number?

B: Of course not. My name is Smith, s-m-i-t-h, and my telephone number is 13564578000.

A: Do you want to order now?

B: No. We will order in the evening.

A: Anything else.

B: Nothing more. Thank you.

A: You're welcome. See you then.

B: See you.

Dialogue 2 At a Chinese restaurant

(A: waiter B: guest C: host)

A: Good evening, sir. Do you want me to get you something to drink while you look at the menu?

C: Yes, please. We'd like to try some Chinese beer. What brand do you recommend?

A: Tsingdao Beer is very popular in China. Would you like to try some?

C: OK. We will take two Tsingdao Beers, very cold, please.

A: Are you ready to order now, sir?

B: Yes. But this is my first visit to China. We love Chinese food, but to tell the truth, I know very much little about it.

C: Well, there are eight main cuisines in China, such as Cantonese food, Sichuan food and Zhejiang food...

B: How is Zhejiang food different from Sichuan food?

C: They are very different. Zhejiang food tends to be fresh and mild, while most Sichuan dishes are spicy and hot.

B: What about Cantonese food?

C: Cantonese food is light and known for its tenderness and freshness.

B: That sounds great, but can we order both of them?

C: Yes, of course.

B: Let's have the Shelled Shrimps with Longjing Tea Leaves, please.

C: It's one of the famous dishes of Hangzhou. It looks nice in shape and color; it is very delicious.

B: And also the Fish-Flavor Shredded Pork, please.

C: It is typical of Sichuan style.

B: Is it cooked with fish?

A: No. It has nothing to do with fish, but it is cooked with special fixings and condiments. So it tastes like fish.

B: Great! And here is a chicken and mushroom soup. Do you think the soup is tasty?

A: Yes. And I think that is enough for you. If you want anything else later, just call the waiter.

B: That's right! You're so considerate.

A: I hope you will enjoy the meal.

C: Thank you.

Dialogue 3 At an English restaurant

(A: waiter B: guest)

A: Good evening. Will it be a table for four, sir?

B: Yes, I'm Alan Brown. I booked a table for six people at 7:15, and two more people are on their way.

A: I have your reservation, Mr. Brown. The table will be ready for you at 7:15. It's just 7:00 o'clock. Would you care to have a drink in the bar in the meantime? The bar is to your right. Shall I ask your friends to join you there?

B: That's fine.

A: (The other couple arrive.) Good evening! Is it Mr. Brown's party?

B: Yes, we are.

A: They're in the bar, sir. It's to the right.

(After a few minutes.)

A: Your table is ready, Mr. Brown. Would you please come this way?

B:Thank you.

A:Would you take your seats, please, ladies and gentlemen? (She polls out the seats for them and they sit down.) Do you care for anything to drink before you order?

B:No, thank you. I think we'll skip the appetizer and order straight away.

A:OK, here are your menus.

B:Now let's see...

A:(After waiting for a few minutes.) Are you ready to order now?

B:No, we are still looking at the menu. Maybe you could recommend something for the main course?

A:Certainly. The T-bone Steak is very good. I would suggest you try that.

B:That's a good idea. I love beefsteaks. I'll have the T-bone Steak.

A:What kind of potatoes would you like to go with it?

B:Baked, please.

A:And what will your vegetable be?

B:I'll have the carrots and broccoli.

A:And what would like for an appetizer?

B:I'll have the hor d'oeuvres and the baked salmon.

A:And what do you want to drink?

B:A bottle of wine.

A:And would you like dessert or cheese?

B:Dessert.

A:What can I get you for dessert?

B:I'll take the ice cream. Strawberry ice cream,

A:Thank you.

Vocabulary

soy sauce	酱油
vinegar	醋
green onion	葱
ginger	姜
garlic	蒜
chili pepper	辣椒
MSG =monosodium glutamate	味精
pepper	胡椒
curry	咖喱
mustard	芥末
ketchup	番茄酱
olive oil	橄榄油
onion	洋葱
red pepper powder	甜椒粉
chili sauce	辣椒酱
meat diet	荤菜
vegetables	素菜
meat broth	肉羹
local dish	地方菜
Cantonese cuisine	广东菜
set meal	客饭
boiling	煮
stewing	煲/炖
braising	烧/焖/烩
frying	煎
stir-frying	炒
quick-frying	爆

deep-frying	炸
frying and simmering	扒
sauteing	煸
simmering	煨
smoking	熏
roasting/barbecuing	烤
baking	烘
steaming	蒸
scalding	白灼

Useful Expressions

1. Making invitations

(1) Would you like to have dinner with me tonight?

(2) I was wondering if you felt like going to have dinner tonight?

(3) How about going out to dinner?

(4) How do you like to come to my housewarming party tomorrow night?

(5) Do you feel like going to taking a harbor cruise?

(6) Do you want to spend the holiday with us?

(7) How do you like to have a tea with me?

2. Accepting an invitation

(1) Yes, of course.

(2) Yes, with pleasure.

(3) Yes, I'd love to.

(4) Yes, I'd like to very much.

(5) Yes, that sounds nice.

(6) Yes, that's a good idea.

(7) Yes, I like the idea.

3. Declining an invitation politely

(1) It's nice of you to ask, but I don't think I can.

(2) I'd love to, but honestly, I really can't.

(3) I won't be able to, I'm afraid, but thanks all the same.

(4) I'm afraid I'm busy then. Can't we make it another day?

(5) I'm sorry, but I can't. What about anther time?

(6) I'm awfully sorry, but I really must finish my work tonight

(7) I hope you don't mind, but I just don't feel up to it tonight.

(8) I'd really like to, but I just can't, I'm afraid.

4. Eating at the restaurant

(1) Could you arrange me a table now?

(2) Have you got a table for two, please?

(3) Have you booked a table?

(4) Have you made a reservation?

(5) Would you care to have a drink in the lounge while waiting?

(6) Would you like to see the menu?

(7) May I order a glass of wine?

(8) What do you recommend?

(9) Anything good for this evening?

(10) What would you like to have?

(11) Is there anything else you would like to have?

(12) What is the specialty of the house?

(13) Do you have today's speciality?

(14) May I take your order?

(15) What would you like to go with your steak?

(16) Could you give us a brief description of the Chinese food?

(17) We have no idea of the food here, Can you recommend some to us?

(18) What soup do you like?

(19) Our restaurant features Shanghai style and Guangdong style.

(20) Can I have the bill, please?

(21) Here is the bill. The total amount is...

(22) Altogether two hundred and twenty Yuan.

(23) Let me have a look at the bill.

(24) Does it include the service charge?

(25) Here is your change.

5. Talking about cooking

(1) How is the taste?

(2) It smells good.

(3) The cake is the best that I've ever had.

(4) Sichuan food is too hot for me.

(5) The dish tastes kind of stale.

(6) The soup is too heavily seasoned.

(7) The beef is too tough.

(8) I'd like to propose a toast to our distinguished guests.

(9) May I propose a toast to our friendship and friendly cooperation?

(10) Here's a toast to your promotion.

(11) Here's to your health.

(12) Don't stand on ceremony.

(13) I can't reach that dish. Could you turn around the lazy Susan?

(14) Tom treats me to seafood.

(15) Chinese food is characterized by its color, aroma and flavor.

(16) Sichuan cuisine is known for its hot flavors.

(17) Cantonese are known to have an adventurous palate, able to eat many different kinds of meats and vegetables.

(18) In general, in addition to flavors, Chinese cuisine gives special attention to the food's nutrition, colors and textures.

Exercises

1. Practice making invitations with a partner like this. A sample dialogue is below for your reference.

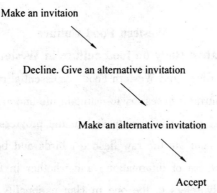

Make an invitaion

Decline. Give an alternative invitation

Make an alternative invitation

Accept

Sample dialogue

A: Would you like to have a dinner with me this Friday evening?

B: Oh, I'd love to, but I'm afraid I'm visiting a client.

A: What a pity. Well, how about this Saturday afternoon then? I really look forward to having a discussion about this product with you.

B: Saturday would be quite fine.

A: Oh, great! I'll pick you up at your hotel at 3 p.m. Does that suit you?

B: Sure, it's quite OK. Thank you. See you this Saturday then.

A: See you. Have a nice day.

2. Work with your partner to role-play

(1) Inviting your business associate to dinner. (accepting)

(2) Asking your friend to go picnicking. (declining)

(3) Inviting your colleague to go on a tour to Hawaii. (first declining, but accepting after persisting)

(4) Imagine that you are at a restaurant with a foreign visitor who doesn't know about Chinese food. Recommend some local specialties, describe what they are, how to eat them and tell the way to cook them.

(5) Suppose that you and your partner are planning a dinner out for eight people. The spending budget is about 500 Yuan. You have a book a table in a restaurant and make out a list of the dishes you would like to have a dinner.

Supplementary Reading

Western Food Culture
A Comparative study on food culture in Western and China

1. Introduce the food in China and Western Food, as essential prerequisite for existence, is any substance that provides the nutrients necessary to maintain life and growth when ingested. It plays an irreplaceable role in the development of society and in the progress of human beings, whether in ancient times when primitive man ate the raw flesh o f birds and beasts or in modern times when humans have entered the new era of information, and whether in East or in West. Chinese food culture in this research mainly refers to the one in Han nationality. As we all know, China is a nation with 56 ethnic groups, each of which has its unique food, food habits, etc. But the Han nationality and its culture are the mainstream in China due to some historical, political and economic reasons, which, however, are not the main concerns of this research. Besides, the author which is much more familiar to the Han cultural background, than that of any other ethnic group. Western food culture in this research is mainly concerned with the one in the English-speaking countries, especially in America and Britain due to the fact that their cultural patterns and influence have become dominant in the West, which is generally recognized by the international community. On the other hand, most of the materials and information on food culture collected by the author are all about American or British people's food, food habits, etc. There are great disparities between China and Western countries in etiquette and content of food cultures, so the comparative study of Chinese & Western food cultures will help us increase cross-cultural awareness that tolerating, understanding, and furthermore, appreciating and respecting cultural difference is essential if we are to achieve cross-cultural competence during the interaction. Moreover, as we communicate with people from different cultures, we will learn more about them and their way of life, including their history, values and the substance of their personality, and eventually, we will understand them better, or feel empathy with them. Based on the above-mentioned purposes, the author of this thesis hopes this research, to some extent, be of significance both theoretically and practically.

2. Comparison of Food Culture between China and West from Table. As we know, the people

regard food as of fundamental importance. Every country has their own food culture. So this thesis mainly introduces the differences between China and Western culture from culture and differences. The main difference between Chinese and Western eating habits is that unlike the West, where everyone has their own plate of food, in China the dishes are placed on the table and everybody share s. If you are being treated by a Chinese host, you will be prepared for a ton of food. Chinese are very proud of their culture of food and will do their best to give you a taste of many different types of cuisine. Among friends, they will just order enough for the people there. If they are taking somebody out for dinner and the relation ship is polite to semi-polite, then they will usually order one more dish than the number of guests. If it is a business dinner or a very formal occasion, there is likely to be a huge amount of food that will be impossible to finish. Traditionally speaking, there are many prohibitions at Chinese tables, but these days not many people pay attention to them. However, there are a few things to keep in mind, especially if you are a guest at a private home. But you'd better remember these things: (1) Don't stick your chopsticks upright in the rice bowl. Instead, lay them on your dish. The reason for this is that when somebody dies, the shrine to them contains a bowl of sand or rice with two sticks of incense stuck upright in it. So if you stick your chopsticks in the rice bowl, it looks like this shrine and is equivalent to wishing death upon a person at the table! (2) Make sure the spout of the teapot is not facing anyone. It is impolite to set the teapot down where the spout is facing towards somebody. The spout should always be directed to where nobody is sitting, usually just outward from the table. (3) Don't tap on your bowl with your chopsticks. Beggars tap on their bowls, so this is not polite. Also, in a restaurant, if the food is coming too slow people will tap their bowls. If you are in someone' s home, it is like insulting the cook. In my opinion, realizing the differences between China and Western country, Chinese combine the acceptable part that makes our daily food richful, but china never lose own characters, which is the correct.

3. A brief discussion of cultural differences between Chinese and Western restaurants Food and beverage products as a result of geographical features, climate environment, customs and other factors, will appear in the raw materials, flavors, cooking methods, eating habits of different degrees of difference. It is precisely because of these differences, food and beverage products have a strong regional. The difference between Chinese and Western cultures to create a diet of Chinese and Western cultural differences, and this difference from the Western way of thinking and a different philosophy of life. Chinese people focus on "harmony between man and nature", the Western

emphasis on "people-oriented."

4. The culture of food and dining in the West is a little different from that in China. The proper western dinner at a fine restaurant is one of manners, focusing on conversation. You are expected to have knowledge of table manners such as what folk or knife to use as these are essential in western dining. The meal would consist of several courses including a soup or salad, an appetizer, the main dish, and a dessert. The atmosphere will be filled with light music that would only serve as background as people converse with each other. The decorations are usually sparse and are only meant to highlight the atmosphere that is being created by the music. This type of dining is different from the dining experience in most restaurants in China. However, with the increase in internationalism, more restaurants are opening which reflect the more western dining style. The Chinese people, now more affluent and knowledgeable about international customs, are beginning to join in this dining experience. This is not to say that people have given up the deep richness in culture that Chinese food represents. It only means that more choices and tastes are becoming available to population. This represents a significant improvement as it will change the perception that the height of western dining is fast food. As cultural communication expands, knowledge of western food will improve.

Chapter 13

Business Travel

Warm-up Exercise

1. Translate the following passage into Chinese

Business travel is the practice of people travelling for purposes related to their work. It is on the rise especially with foreign business markets opening up. 432 million business trips were completed by United States residents in 2009, this accounted for approximately $215 billion dollars towards the economy.

Many airlines began to concentrate on providing premium service on long haul flights especially for the first and business class business traveller with the development of more sophisticated business traveller needs over the last 15 years.

American Airlines was the first airline to offer a frequent flier program to customers. The advantage program began in May 1981 and included Hertz car rental and Hyatt hotel. The first hotel to start an independent hotel program was Holiday Inn; they began in January 1983. National Car Rental was the first car rental company to introduce a program back in March 1987. Airlines have also been working on tools that benefit the business travellers such as: Improved and competitive mileage programs, quick check in and online check in, lounges with broadband connection, etc. Hotels are not far behind. They are also on the competition for the business travellers by offering flexible points programs, broadband connection in all rooms and fast check in and check out services.

While internet booking engines have become the first destination for around 60% of leisure travellers, business travellers, especially with the need for itineraries that may include more than one destination, have still found that a knowledgeable travel agent may be their best resource for better ticket pricing, less hassle and better air and land travel planning. For larger business travel accounts these travel agents take on a travel management role, and are referred to as Travel Management Companies (TMCs), providing services such as consultancy, traveller tracking, data and negotiation assistance and policy advice.

Recent trends in this market have extended to the implementation of Self Booking Tools (SBTs) which allow automated booking of trips within company policy, an increase in the inclusion of Duty of care practices in the booking and monitoring process and more consideration for the environmental impact of business travel.

Top three expense categories for business travel:
● Airline expenses
● Hotel expenses
● Food and beverage expenses

2. Do you happen to know any regulations for taking a plane? Tick the statements you think are true

(　　) (1) Passengers can only hand-carry a small bag aboard the plane.
(　　) (2) Children under 5 needn't buy a ticket.
(　　) (3) People who haven't got an ID card cannot board the plane.
(　　) (4) Passengers mustn't carry dangerous articles such as compressed gases, weapons, explosives, corrosives, or inflammables onto the plane.
(　　) (5) Passengers can smoke during the flight.
(　　) (6) Passengers mustn't use mobile telephones on flights because they will interfere with the plane's electronic equipment.
(　　) (7) Passengers must check in 30 minutes before departure on international flights.
(　　) (8) Passengers must fasten their seat belts during take-off or landing.
(　　) (9) The airline needn't accept responsibility for delays due to bad weather.
(　　) (10) Passengers can transfer their tickets to others without going to the booking office.

Sample Dialogues

Dialogue 1

A: Air China. May I help you?

B: Yes, I'd like to make reservations on your flight number 220, departing for New York on December 22nd at 7:00 in the evening.

A: Your name, please?

B: Mr. William Robert and Mrs. Jane Robert.

A: Do you want to fly first or economy class?

B: Economy.

A: Yes, we still have room on that flight. Will this be a one-way trip?

B: No, round trip back to Beijing on January 3rd. By the way, do you have any direct flights coming back?

A: Yes, we do. Flight number 532, leaving New York at 3:00 in the afternoon, flies nonstop back to Beijing.

B: That'll be perfect. What is the exact air fare?

A: Economy fare round trip from Beijing to New York is $2030 during peak season.

B: I see... Then our tickets are confirmed?

A: Yes, your seats are confirmed on those two flights. Please be at the airport at least one hour before departure time.

Dialogue 2

A: Miss, would you give me your ticket and passport, please?

B: Here you are.

A: Window seat or aisle seat?

B: Window seat, please. By the way, I'm a little bit airsick. Is it possible to put me in the front?

A: Sure. Would you like to check any luggage?

B: Yes, I'd like to check three pieces.

A: Could you label your luggage and put it on the scales, please?

B: OK.

A: I'm afraid your luggage is overweight.

B: How much luggage can I carry?

A: As a rule, the free luggage allowance for an economy ticket is 20 kilos. Now your baggage is 25kilos. I'm afraid you have to pay an excess luggage charge.

B: What's the overweight charge per kilo?

A: Twenty dollars.

B: OK. Here's 100 dollars. By the way, can I keep this small bag as hand luggage?

A: Sure. Here's your ticket and boarding pass. Have a pleasant flight.

B: Thank you.

Dialogue 3

A: May I see your passport, please?

B: Here is my passport. And this is the declaration form.

A: What is the purpose of your visit to the United States?

B: Business. I have a trade conference to attend in Chicago.

A: This visa is good for two weeks. Do you intend to stay longer than that?

B: No. I will fly back twelve days from now.

A: And you will do some travelling while you are here?

B: Yes, I want to spend a couple of days in New York. I have friends there I will visit.

A: What do you have in the bag, Mr. Lee?

B: Just my cameras, my clothes and some books.

A: You're not carrying any food with you today?

B: No.

A: Ok. Mr. Lee. This is just a routine check. Would you mind opening the bag for me?

B: Alright.

A: Hmm. You have three cameras. Are you a photographer?

B: No, my company makes cameras. Well, I'm also a photographer, but two of these are for out display.

A: I see. And what's in this bag?

B: Egg tarts.

A: I thought you said you didn't have any food with you today.

B: I thought you meant vegetables and meat when you asked me. Things like that. I don't have any vegetables.

A: I'm sorry, Mr. Lee. Egg tarts are food too. We will have to take them away.

B: Take them away?

A: Yes, we will have to dispose of them.

B: It's too bad. They are very delicious.

A: I know. One out of every three travellers from Hong Kong seems to be carrying them. They are being smuggled in by a lot of people.

B: Oh, well. Not by me.

A: No, not today at least. Enjoy your visit to the United States, Mr. Lee.

B: Thank you.

Dialogue 4

A: Good afternoon.

B: I'd like to book a double room for Tuesday next week.

A: That's fine, sir. A double room for Tuesday, September 12th, with a front view or rear view?

B: What's the price difference?

A: A double room with a front view is 140 dollars per night, one with a rear view is 115 dollars per night.

B: I think I'll take the one with a front view then.

A: How long will you be staying?

B: We'll be leaving Sunday morning.

A: That will be five nights, sir. Thank you very much, and we look forward to seeing you next Tuesday.

B: Good. That's all settled then. Good-bye.

A: Good-bye.

Dialogue 5

A: I've got a reservation here. My name is John Sandals.

B: Mr. Sandals, may I see your ID, please?

A: One second, please, while I dig it out. Here.

B: Now, sir, do you have a credit card?

A: Yes, I do. Do you accept American Express?

B: I'm sorry, Mr. Sandals, but we accept only Master Card or VISA.

A: That's okay, I've got plenty of cards. Here's my VISA.

B: Okay. You're in room 507. It's a single queen-size bed, spacious, and nonsmoking. Is that suitable?

A: Yes, that's just what I wanted.

B: Here's your key, sir. If you need anything, just dial 0 on your room phone.

Dialogue 6

A: Good morning, sir. Can I help you?

B: I'd like to pay my bill now.

A: Your name and room number, please?

B: George Wright, Room 706.

A: Yes, Mr. Wright. Have you used any hotel service this morning?

B: No, I haven't used any services.

A: Fine. This is your bill, Mr. Wright. That makes a total of 665 U.S. dollars.

B: Can I pay by credit card?

A: Certainly. May I have your card, please?

B: Here you are.

A: Please sign your name here.

B: Oh, yes. Is it possible to leave my luggage here until I'm ready to leave this afternoon? I'd like to say good-bye to some of my friends.

A: Yes, we'll keep it for you. How many pieces of your luggage?

B: Just three. I'll be back by 3:00.

A: That's fine. Have a nice day.

B: Thank you. See you later.

Key terms

international flight	国际班机
flight number	班机号码
round-trip ticket	来回机票
business class	商务客舱
domestic flight	国内班机
one-way ticket	单程机票
first class	头等舱
economy class	经济舱
laboratory	盥洗室
occupied	使用中
vacant	无人
stewardess	女空服员
steward	男空服员
customs service area	海关申报处
currency declaration	货币申报
duty-free items	免税商品
dutiable goods	需课税商品
sightseeing	观光
baggage/luggage	行李
checked baggage	托运的行李
baggage claim area	行李领取处
carry-on baggage	随身行李
baggage tag	行李牌
luggage cart	行李推车
currency exchange shop	外币兑换店
exchange rate	汇率

traveller's check	旅行支票
room rate	房价
standard rate	标准价
en-suite	套房
family suite	家庭套房
advance deposit	定金
reservation	订房间
registration	登记
rate sheets	房价表
tariff	价目表
cancellation	取消预定
imperial suite	皇室套房
presidential suite	总统套房
suite deluxe	高级套房
junior suite	简单套房
mini suite	小型套房
honeymoon suite	蜜月套房
penthouse suite	楼顶套房
unmade room	未清扫房
on change	待清扫房
valuables	贵重品
porter	行李员
luggage/baggage	行李
registered/checked luggage	托运行李
light luggage	轻便行李
baggage elevator	行李电梯
form	表格
reservation	预订
reception desk	待处
tip	小费

reservation desk	预订处
luggage office	行李房
registration desk	宿登记处
lobby	前厅
luggage rack	行李架
visit card	名片
identification card	身份证
rate of exchange	兑换率
conversion rate	换算率
change money	换钱
information desk	问询处
luggage label	行李标签
overbooking	超额订房
procedure fee	手续费
fill in the form	填表
twin room	带两张单人床的房间
double room	带一张双人床的房间

Useful Expressions

1. May I see your passport, please?
2. How long are you going to stay in America?
3. I will stay for one week.
4. What is the purpose of your visit?
5. Do you have anything to declare?
6. I have nothing to declare.
7. Excuse me, where is the baggage claim area?
8. Where is the lost luggage office?

9. Where can I get a luggage cart?

10. I'd like to change NT＄10 000 into U.S. Dollars, please.

11. Can you tell me where to change money?

12. Can you accept travellers' checks?

13. What's the exchange rate?

14. I'd like to change NT＄10,000 into U.S. Dollars, please.

15. How much luggage are you checking in?

16. Do you have a carry-on?

17. Can you place your baggage up here?

18. Your luggage is overweight.

19. Single or return?

20. Do you prefer window or aisle?

21. We do not have any aisle seats remaining. Is a window seat OK with you or would you prefer a middle seat?

22. Do you have a seat next to the emergency exit?

23. Here are your tickets. The gate number is on the bottom of the ticket.

24. They will start boarding 20 minutes before the departure time. You should report to gate C2 by then.

25. How much is a return ticket?

26. How many pieces of luggage can I take with me?

27. The free allowance for baggage is 20 kilos.

28. I'd like to book a business class ticket on Cathay Pacific Flight 808 to Paris.

29. Are you a member of the frequent flyer program?

30. Can you sign me up for a frequent flyer program?

31. Will you please give me your ticket and passport?

32. I'm afraid you have to pay an excess luggage charge.

33. Here's your boarding card/pass, ticket and passport.

34. Is your luggage properly labeled?

35. Please put your watch, mobile phone, and keys into this small basket before you go through

the security gate.

36. Would you put your luggage on the conveyor belt and have it X-rayed?
37. Those who haven't got anything to declare, please go through the Green Pass.
38. Please fill in this Customs Declaration Form.
39. How much should I pay for the duty?
40. Is there a room available for tonight?
41. No, all the rooms are booked for tonight.
42. Do you have a room for tonight?
43. I reserved a room for tonight.
44. I'd like to book a double room for Tuesday next week.
45. I'd like a single room from the 6th for three nights.
46. I'd like to reserve a suite from the 18th for five nights.
47. Do you have any vacancies for the night of the 13th?
48. What's your rate?
49. Does this include breakfast?
50. A double room with a front view is 140 dollars per night, one with a rear view is 115 dollars per night.
51. I think I'll take the one with a front view then.
52. How long will you be staying?
53. Could I see your passport?
54. Could you please fill in this registration form?
55. I'm checking out.
56. Can I have your key and room number, please?
57. Here's your bill, sir. Could you please check it?
58. It's all right. Please charge it to my credit card.
59. Here you are, sir. You're all set. I hope you enjoyed your stay.

Exercises

1. Situational talks

(1) Suppose you work in the administration department of a company, and there is guest coming to visit your company next Wednesday and Thursday. Please book a room for him.

(2) Your boss is going to attend the Shanghai APEC CEO Summit next month. As his secretary, you are responsible for the planning of his trip. Now phone the booking office of an airline to make the reservation to Shanghai for a set date.

(3) You have arrived at a hotel now. You are now busy checking in at the hotel reception desk.

(4) You are at an airport. You have just finished checking in and are proceeding to the security check. Suppose you are carrying a toy gun for your son and a bottle of styling mousse.

(5) Suppose you are on a business trip, you may make reservations for flights through telephone, check in at the airport, get on board and travel by air, and put yourself up at a certain hotel. You are required to make situational dialogues with your partner on the above-mentioned several steps. During the whole process, you and your partner may exchange roles.

(6) You are going on a business trip to Sydney next week. Work with your partner and make up dialogues for the following situations

● Booking a round-trip ticket from Hong Kong to Sydney

● Postponing the flight because for an important meeting

● Checking in at the airport

● Going through the security check

● Going through customs

2. Complete the following dialogues by translating the Chinese in the brackets

(1) A: Good evening, sir. Welcome to our hotel.

　　B: Good evening. _____.(我在你们酒店订了一个单人房间。)

　　A: Single room. Let me check. _____.(哦, 有了。您的房间号是

8642,这是您的房卡。)

......

A:_____.(请把护照给我,并请填上这份旅客登记表。)

(2) A:Beijing Sheraton. Can I help you?

B:_____?(请你接格林先生好吗?)

A:May I have this room number?

B:_____.(哦,抱歉。我不知道他的房间号码。)

A:_____.(请别挂上电话。约翰·格林先生的房间是8642号,请您同他讲话吧。)

B:Thanks a lot.

(3) A:_____?(您想留个口信吗?)

B:No._____.(过半个小时我再打个电话试试。)

(4) A: Good morning, sir. What can I do for you?

B: My room number is 8642. I'd like to _____.(再续住两天。)

Supplementary Reading

Chinese cuisine

A number of different styles contribute to Chinese cuisine, but perhaps the best known and most influential are Guangdong (Cantonese) cuisine, Shandong cuisine, Jiangsu cuisine and Sichuan cuisine. These styles are distinctive from one another due to factors such as available resources, climate, geography, history, cooking techniques and lifestyle. One style may favor the use of lots of garlic and shallots over lots of chilli and spices, while another may favor preparing seafood over other meats and fowl. Jiangsu cuisine favors cooking techniques such as braising and stewing, while Sichuan cuisine employs baking, just to name a few. Hairy crab is a highly sought after local delicacy in Shanghai, as it can be found in lakes within the region. Beijing Roast Duck (otherwise known as "Peking Duck") is another popular dish well known outside of China. Based on the raw materials and ingredients used, the method of preparation and cultural differences, a variety of foods with different flavors and textures are prepared in different regions of the country. Many traditional regional cuisines rely on basic methods of preservation such as drying, salting, pickling and fermentation.

Chuan (Sichuan)

Szechuan cuisine, also called Sichuan cuisine, is a style of Chinese cuisine originating in the Sichuan Province of southwestern China famed for bold flavors, particularly the pungency and spiciness resulting from liberal use of garlic and chili peppers, as well as the unique flavor of the Sichuan peppercorn (花椒) and zhitianjiao (指天椒). Peanuts, sesame paste and ginger are also prominent ingredients in Szechuan cooking.

Hui (Anhui)

Anhui cuisine (Chinese: 徽菜 or 安徽菜) is one of the Eight Culinary Traditions of China. It is derived from the native cooking styles of the Huangshan Mountains region in China and is similar to Jiangsu cuisine. But it emphasizes less on seafood and more on a wide variety of local herbs and vegetables. Anhui province is particularly endowed with fresh bamboo and mushroom crops.

Lu (Shandong)

Shandong Cuisine is commonly and simply known as Lu cuisine. With a long history, Shandong Cuisine once formed an important part of the imperial cuisine and was widely promoted in North China. However, it isn't so popular in South China and even in the all-embracing Shanghai.

Shandong Cuisine is featured by a variety of cooking techniques and seafood. The typical dishes on local menu are braised abalone, braised trepang, sweet and sour carp, Jiuzhuan Dachang and Dezhou Chicken. Various Shandong snacks are also worth trying.

Min (Fujian)

Fujian cuisine is a traditional Chinese cuisine. Many diverse seafoods are used, including hundreds of types of fish, shellfish and turtles, provided by the Fujian coastal region. Woodland delicacies such as edible mushrooms and bamboo shoots are also utilized. Slicing techniques are valued in the cuisine and utilized to enhance the flavor, aroma and texture of seafood and other foods. Fujian cuisine is often served in a broth or soup, with cooking techniques including braising, stewing, steaming and boiling.

Su (Jiangsu, Huaiyang cuisine)

Jiangsu cuisine, also known as Su (Cai) Cuisine for short, is one of the major components of Chinese cuisine, which consists of the styles of Yangzhou, Nanjing, Suzhou and Zhenjiang dishes. It is very famous all over the world for its distinctive style and taste. It is especially popular in the lower reach of the Yangtze River.

Typical courses of Jiangsu cuisine are Jinling salted dried duck (Nanjing's most famous dish), crystal meat (pork heels in a bright, brown sauce), clear crab shell meatballs (pork meatballs in crab shell powder, fatty, yet fresh), Yangzhou steamed Jerky strips (dried tofu, chicken, ham and pea leaves), triple combo duck, dried duck, and Farewell My Concubine (soft-shelled turtle stewed with many other ingredients such as chicken, mushrooms and wine).

Yue (Hong Kong and Guangdong)

Dim sum, literally "touch your heart", is a Cantonese term for small hearty dishes. These bite-sized portions are prepared using traditional cooking methods such as frying, steaming, stewing and baking. It is designed so that one person may taste a variety of different dishes. Some of these may include rice rolls, lotus leaf rice, turnip cakes, buns, shui jiao-style dumplings, stir-fried green vegetables, congee porridge, soups, etc. The Cantonese style of dining, yum cha, combines the variety of dim sum dishes with the drinking of tea. Yum cha literally means "drink tea". Cantonese style is the unique and charm dishes, which enjoy a long history and a good reputation both at home and abroad. It is common with other parts of the diet and cuisine in Chinese food culture. Back in ancient times, and the Central Plains on Lingnan Yue Chu family has close contacts. With the changes of dynasty historically, many people escaped the war and crossed the Central Plains, the increasing integration of the two communities. Central Plains culture gradually moved to the south. As a result, their food production techniques, cookware, utensils and property turned into a rich combination of Agriculture, which is the origin of Cantonese food. Cantonese cuisine originated in the Han.

Xiang (Hunan)

Hunan cuisine is well known for its hot spicy flavor, fresh aroma and deep color. Common cooking techniques include stewing, frying, pot-roasting, braising, and smoking. Due to the high agricultural output of the region, there are varied ingredients for Hunan dishes.

Zhe (Zhejiang)

Zhejiang cuisine (Chinese: 浙菜 or 浙江菜), one of the Eight Culinary Traditions of China, derives from the native cooking styles of the Zhejiang region. The dishes are not greasy, having but instead a fresh, soft flavor with a mellow fragrance.

The cuisine consists of at least three styles, each of which originates from different cities in the province:

Hangzhou style, characterized by rich variations and the use of bamboo shoots.

Shaoxing style, specializing in poultry and freshwater fish.

Ningbo style, specializing in seafood.